M000119907

Beauty Inside Out relates spiritual truths to beauty and makeup and helps you learn to prioritize becoming beautiful in God's sight. I have been in the beauty business as a leader, teacher, and motivator for forty years, and I have never seen a book like this! I can't wait to send copies to all my friends.

—Karen Piro, executive independent national sales director emeritus, Mary Kay Cosmetics

Beauty Inside Out is written in a style that will surely capture the attention of girls both young and old. This twenty-one-day devotional is a wonderful tool that teaches practical truths found in the Word of God in a simple, easy-to-understand format that will inspire all of us to strive for that inner beauty as we seek to enhance our outer beauty.

—Dianne Forrest, pastor of Cornerstone Faith Assembly

Beauty Inside Out is a refreshing and fun devotional that not only makes the Word of God alive and relevant to the reader, but it's also sure to help her remember what she's learned each and every time she engages in her daily beauty routine.

—Dr. Sue Gregg, founder and senior pastor of Bethlehem Christian Fellowship and Bible Training Center

In four transformational weeks, *Beauty Inside Out* uses object lessons to teach spiritual truths and helps you learn to prioritize becoming beautiful in God's sight.

—Hazel Parker Stanley, gospel recording artist and pastor of Cornerstone Ministries, Hackensack, NJ

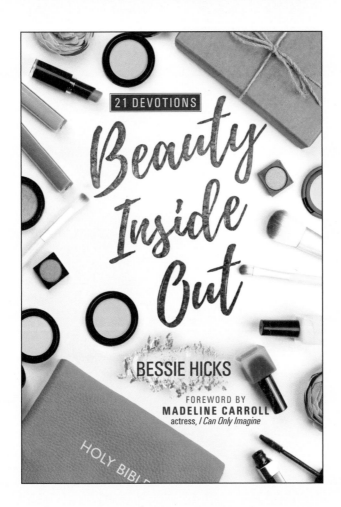

21 DEVOTIONS

Beauty Inside Out

BESSIE HICKS

FOREWORD BY
MADELINE CARROLL
actress, *I Can Only Imagine*

BroadStreet
PUBLISHING

BroadStreet Publishing® Group, LLC
Savage, Minnesota, USA
BroadStreetPublishing.com

Beauty Inside Out: 21 DEVOTIONS

Stock or custom editions of BroadStreet Publishing titles may be purchased in bulk for educational, business, ministry, fundraising, or sales promotional use. For information, please email info@broadstreetpublishing.com.

Cover and interior by Garborg Design at GarborgDesign.com

Printed in China

19 20 21 22 23 5 4 3 2 1

Contents

Foreword

I couldn't wait to read *Beauty Inside Out* when I first got my hands on it because of who wrote it. Once I began reading, I couldn't put it down because of how powerful it was. Each day left me wanting more as I began to learn about myself. The book points to Jesus, of course, but it also pointed out a lot of things in me, such as the way I do things and the way I see myself, which isn't always the best. It showed me the way God sees me, how He wired me, and the way I should see myself. In the pages of this book, you will find truth—and as the Bible says, "'The truth will make you free'" (John 8:32).

I first met Bessie a few years ago at a women's conference while I was on a holiday break. I go to the same place every Christmas, and I should have already been home by that point. But that year, as God had it, I was still there at the very beginning of January. It turned out to be a moment in my life I won't forget. You see, I have been acting since I was just three years old and had a very successful career. I did commercials, television, and lead roles in major motion pictures. I was on my way to stardom when everything came to a crashing halt.

Many people believe Hollywood and faith don't mix, and I was finding that to be very true. I love God, and I wasn't willing to compromise my faith. When I became a teenager, suddenly there were no longer any normal roles. The content of scripts had changed, so I came to a point where I questioned my calling. I felt as if I'd lost my identity. Was acting no longer what God had for me? The opposition was too much with everyone around me telling me it was impossible to hold on to my dream. They said it would never work out because Hollywood would never change!

Then came Bessie.

In a way, God moved heaven and earth for me to meet her. He knew she would be the willing vessel to speak life to me and to my dream. I remember watching her go up to the pulpit, and having never heard her preach before, I wondered what she would say. I desperately needed to hear from God, and I've found when you're already in that posture, God speaks. Of course, I know God is always speaking, but when we need Him badly, He finds a way to make Himself clear to us.

That day He delivered His message through Bessie. She "preached the walls down" (one of Bessie's favorite statements). She was a powerhouse. She pointed right at me that day during her sermon and said, "God always raises up one from among them." It was a moment I'll never forget. I cried because I knew the Holy Spirit spoke through her. Even then, I had a feeling that carrying out this challenge wasn't going to be easy, but I had to accept it. God had raised me up from among them (Hollywood), and my purpose was to lead people out and toward Jesus.

I left church that day telling all my friends I had a new favorite preacher—and her name was Bessie Hicks.

God moved our worlds around to be in that moment together. The words she spoke kept me going, and I began expectantly waiting for her new sermons to come out. I felt connected to her. Bessie is like that—you're drawn in within just a few minutes. Her love for God pours from her lips. I still haven't found anyone who knows the Word like her, rattling off passages as if telling you her grocery list. Sometimes she preaches purely from the heart and doesn't even need to read from the Bible. The Bible just flows out from her! This is why when I heard she was writing *Beauty Inside Out*, I had to read it immediately. And I recommend you do the same.

It's sometimes hard for us to look in the mirror with all our beauty products on and see ourselves clearly. But I hope you will allow *Beauty Inside Out* to help you see yourself through the mirror of God's Word. You may not like what you see at first, but after spending time in His presence, I promise that you will love the new you!

Madeline Carroll
Actress, *I Can Only Imagine*

Introduction

Beauty Inside Out is a twenty-one-day devotional for women, using beauty products, processes, and treatments to teach spiritual truths. According to 1 Corinthians 15:46, the natural things of this world are understood before the spiritual. Getting a clear understanding of the natural makes it easier to understand the spiritual. As women, there are few things we know better than beauty products. This book has been handcrafted by the Holy Spirit to meet you right where you are. We will use things that are familiar to us as women and make them relatable to the Word of God.

This method of teaching with parables is nothing new. Jesus, the greatest teacher ever, used parables to teach spiritual truths. He taught in this way so we could understand what He was saying. When speaking with fishermen, He used examples of fishing, and when speaking to farmers, He used seeds and sowing. God is so interested in relating to you that He sent His Son, Jesus, into the world as a man. He became like us to redeem and relate to us so we could understand Him.

Maybe you have had a difficult time in the past studying the Word of God. It may have seemed intimidating or even overwhelming to you. If that's the case, then *Beauty Inside Out* was written just for you. Although it's written in a devotional format, it goes much deeper, provoking you to study the Bible and build a relationship with the Lord. Through the pages of this easy-to-understand book you will find the Word of God coming to life.

It is our hope that every morning as you begin your day, simply washing and moisturizing your face will become a reminder of what you have been learning. While you apply your makeup, the importance of having a proper foundation will come back to you. Going to get your hair done or visiting the spa will never be the same, but will become tools that the Lord will use to help you learn and remember biblical truths.

With the Holy Spirit as your teacher and guide, you will begin to see things through the eyes of the Spirit. The hours you spend on making yourself beautiful on the outside will be transformed into daily reminders of the importance of working on your inner beauty. Of course, every woman wants to look beautiful; there's nothing wrong with that. But what about being beautiful in the sight of God—shouldn't that be our top priority?

YOU CAN BE A BEAUTY

Here's some good news: We're not saying you have to be homely to be holy. You can be blood bought as well as beautiful, godly, and gorgeous! The Bible is full of beautiful women who were used by God. Esther 2:7 tells us Esther "had a lovely figure and was beautiful" (NIV). He desires to use your beauty to bring Him glory as He did with Esther.

YOU CAN BE A STAR

In a day and age when everyone wants to be a movie star, Esther is the kind of star we should want to be. She also found favor with the king and risked her life to go before him, pleading for the salvation of her people. The Lord brought her to the kingdom, "for such a time as this" (4:14). Her willingness to submit to her cousin's godly counsel, and her bravery to go before the king (after fasting and prayer) saved a nation. Esther, whose name means "star," shined bright in a dark situation and was used to save many. Doesn't that sound like Jesus!

A TIME SUCH AS THIS

There was an appointed time of preparation that Esther went through to get her ready to receive God's plan for her life. We believe that God has inspired us to write this book for you as a time of preparation. He has a plan for your life, and He wants you ready to receive it. We hope that beginning this inner beauty regiment will form a new habit in your life (or ignite an old one) of regular devotional time and Bible study—lasting long after this book is finished.

FOR MAXIMUM RESULTS, FOLLOW THE INSTRUCTIONS

1. In order to get the most out of your beauty products, you must follow the instructions. The same goes for this devotional. In order to get the most out of it, you must be willing to follow the directions.

2. This book is set up on a Monday through Friday schedule. It is not meant to be a quick read, but rather twenty-one days of laid-out foundational truth. If done correctly (including Bible reading and questions answered), it should take you about twenty to thirty minutes each day.

3. Don't skip the Daily Reflections at the end of each chapter. The reading of the Word is the most important part of this book! There is no book besides the Bible that contains the life-giving power of the Word of God. Jesus said His words are spirit and life (John 6:63). *Beauty Inside Out* is not intended to be a substitute for your Bible but a tool to help in learning and understanding the Word.

This spiritual makeover begins with your willingness to let God transform you through His Word. Let's get started.

*And let the beauty of the L*ORD *our God be upon us.*

—PSALM 90:17

WEEK 1

Skin Care

DAY 1

The Cleanse

Bessie Hicks

*To Him who loved us
and washed us from our sins in His own blood.*

REVELATION 1:5

All beauty regiments should begin with cleansing. Whether it's our skin, hair, or nails, everyone likes a fresh, clean start. When it comes to skin care, we have many options to choose from, and picking the right cleanser for your skin may seem overwhelming at first. Whether you're in a drugstore or a department store, the shelves are packed with products that are full of promises. However, there's one cleansing agent that stands out far and above the rest, that stands behind every promise. You can't purchase this product; rather, you were purchased by it. I'm talking about the blood of Jesus—the only thing that can truly wash you clean!

BEAUTY INSIDER TIP 1

The blood cleanses from the inside out

With health and beauty products, there's always a trending fad. A recent one that has become popular is doing a "cleanse." The purpose of a cleanse, or detox, is to clean your body from the inside and remove built-up toxins that are harmful to your health. One of the many benefits of a detox is clearer skin. The cleaning from the inside affects your appearance on the outside. In other words, making you beautiful from the inside out.

Psalm 139:14 declares we were "fearfully and wonderfully made" by God. He created our natural body with a cleansing agent on the inside—our blood. We can look at how God created the blood in our body and see spiritual truths about the blood of Jesus, and how it cleanses us.

According to Leviticus 17:11, "the life of the flesh is in the blood." Every twenty-three seconds, your heart pumps blood completely through your body. The blood brings oxygen (life) to your cells and organs, then picks up the waste. By waste, I mean all the junk we consume. The blood picks up that waste and brings it to the parts of the body that will dispose of it, cleansing us from the inside out. The blood of Jesus also cleanses us from the inside out, washing away our sin and our guilt and shame.

When you're looking for a good cleanser for your skin, you have plenty of options. However, if you want to be cleansed from your sin, there's only one option: the precious blood of Jesus!

Hebrews 9:22 says, "Without the shedding of blood there is no forgiveness of sins" (ESV).

BEAUTY INSIDER TIP 2

The blood is much more than a cleanser

First Peter 1:18–19 says, "Knowing that you were not redeemed with corruptible things, like silver and gold, ... but with the precious blood of Christ, as of a lamb without blemish and without spot." The word used here to describe the blood of Jesus is *precious*. It means valuable, honorable, or of the highest degree. What makes the blood of Jesus so precious is that it is sinless blood. In the natural, the blood is transferred to the baby through the father. Jesus was the Son of God, having received His perfect, sinless blood from His Father. Then He walked on earth and preserved that blood through living a sinless life and dying a spotless sacrifice for the sins of the whole world.

When John the Baptist introduced Jesus to the world (John 1:29), he declared, "Behold! The Lamb of God who takes away the sin of the world!" John's listeners, the Jews, would have understood his reference to the Lamb of God. Every Jew was required to celebrate Passover, a feast dedicated to remembering when the blood of the lamb was applied to the doorpost of their homes (Exodus 12).

This Old Testament story pointed to a powerful New Testament truth. Just as they applied the blood of the lamb to the doorposts of their homes, and were saved, we can apply the blood of Jesus to our hearts and be saved. If you will put your faith in His blood, you can receive eternal life. The blood cleanses us from our sin, causing us to receive eternal life instead of death

(Romans 6:23). The blood not only cleanses us from our sin, paying the debt we owed. It also brings deliverance, healing, provision, and much more.

"He also brought them out with silver and gold, and there was none feeble among His tribes" (Psalm 105:37).

The psalmist here was retelling the story of how God delivered the children of Israel out of Egypt. If you were to continue reading through Exodus, you would see all that happened after the blood of the lamb was shed.

- **Deliverance**: "He also brought them out." God's people had been in bondage to Pharaoh in Egypt for over four hundred years. Despite many attempts by Moses to get Pharaoh to let the Israelites go, even after nine plagues, he refused. But when the tenth plague came, the death of the firstborn, the blood of the lamb on their doorposts protected them. Once the blood was shed, finally Pharaoh released them. When the blood of Jesus is applied, it brings deliverance from every bondage.

- **Provision**: "He also brought them out with silver and gold." In Exodus 3, when God gave Moses the plan of deliverance for His people, God told him that they would not go out empty-handed. He would give them favor with the Egyptians, and they would hand over their silver, gold, and clothing. The Hebrew women simply followed the instructions of God and asked the Egyptians for their silver and gold, and they willingly handed it over. Philippians 4:19 says, "My God shall supply all your need according to His riches in glory by Christ Jesus." Everything we will ever need has been provided by Christ and the blood He shed on Calvary.

- **Healing**: "He also brought them out with silver and gold, and there was none feeble among His tribes." Of the estimated two to three million people who came out of Egypt that night, not one was feeble. They were all strong. After they slew the lamb and applied the blood to the doorposts, they were instructed to eat the whole lamb. Again, by simply following the Lord's instructions given by Moses, they were all supernaturally healed and strengthened so they were able to make a swift escape out of Egypt.

We could never cover all the benefits of the power of the blood of Jesus in this twenty-one-day study, but we will briefly take a look at a few more.

BEAUTY INSIDER TIP 3

Mix soap with water and apply liberally

Throughout today's study, we have been comparing the blood of Jesus to our cleanser (soap). The Bible also refers to us being cleansed by "the washing of water by the word" (Ephesians 5:26). Everyone knows that soap must be mixed with water before it can be lathered up and applied. Soap and water work best together.

"How can a young man cleanse his way? By taking heed according to Your word" (Psalm 119:9).

The psalmist is asking a question: How can we cleanse our way? He then graciously gives us the answer: by heeding the Word of God. I'm a living testimony that this verse is true. Jesus said in John 18:37, "For this cause I have come into the world, that I should bear witness to the truth." Christ's mission was to bear witness to the truth. My co-mission (the mission that He and I are in together) is also to bear witness to the truth—that the Word of God can cleanse your way. He wants to wash us with the water of the Word.

I was saved at a young age and was raised in church my whole life. However, I still needed my way cleansed. I never had a personal revelation of the Word. I lived in a pattern of knowing what was right in my head but doing wrong in my heart. *But*, when I took heed to the Word of God, when I began to hide His Word in my heart (as described in Psalm 119:11), I stopped doing wrong and started living right.

Taking heed to the Word cleansed my way. When I actually started applying the Word instead of just going to church, it radically changed my life. That's been twenty years ago now. He is still changing me day by day—and I have never turned back, looked back, or stood back. Since then, my life has been about studying and teaching people the truth of the Word of God, following Jesus' instruction to "make disciples of all the nations" (Matthew 28:19). That is why the Lord has been able to use me to minister His Word in so many places, from conferences to kitchen tables. He has called me to teach people the truth of the Word of God, to launch a website, and write this book.

* * *

I'm going to close today's devotion with a story from Reinhard Bonnke, the most successful evangelist of our time. He has seen over 75 million people saved through his ministry.

He told a story at the crusade I attended in Durham, North Carolina. He was invited to do a television interview with experts answering "religious" questions. When he arrived, he realized it was just him, a fiery evangelist, and an atheist.

The atheist said, "Bonnke, you preach there's power in the blood of Jesus, but I don't believe that the blood has any power! The blood of Jesus has been in this world for two thousand years, and the world is worse now than ever. The presence of the blood of Jesus in this world has not made the world better. In fact, it has gotten worse. That's why I say there is no power in the blood!"

Bonnke replied, "There's soap in this world, but many people are still dirty! Let me explain to you how soap works, in case you don't know. If I am dirty and I stand next to a piece of soap, I will not be automatically clean. I wouldn't even be clean if I worked in a soap factory! Mister, if you wanna know how soap works, you gotta reach out with your hand and start to apply it. If you do, you will know there is power in the soap, and so it is with the blood of Jesus! It's not enough to know about it, preach about it, or sing about it."

He continued, "Now, Mister, I dare you to reach out for the blood, apply it to your sinful life. If you do, what will happen to you is what has already happened to hundreds of millions of people all over the world! You will find out there is power in the blood!"

Daily Reflection

Read 1 John 1:7-9

- If we confess our sin, He is faithful and just to do what?

Read Revelation 12:11; Ephesians 1:7; Romans 5:9

- What are some of the benefits we receive by the blood of Jesus?

Read Psalm 119:9

- What happens when you take heed to the Word of God?

Application

Romans 10:9 says that "if you confess with your mouth the Lord Jesus and believe in your heart that God raised Him from the dead, you will be saved." Right where you're at, you can simply pray, *Lord, I accept what you did for me on the cross, I believe you rose from the dead. I put my faith in your blood. Come and wash me clean from all my sin. I receive you today.*

If you are reading this book and have already been saved, praise God! Now we can soak in His presence.

DAY 2

The Soak

Bessie Hicks & Annie Smith

He who dwells in the secret place of the Most High
shall abide under the shadow of the Almighty.

PSALM 91:1

I love to soak in the bath at nighttime. It's not just about taking a bath—it's a whole experience. It's so relaxing to lock the door, fill the tub with hot water, add my favorite bath bomb, and hide away for a while. It really is my favorite thing to do after a long day. For me it's like a mini retreat and an escape. I find that it helps me to relax, unwind, and recoup for the next day. Life can get busy, and we don't stop to take time for ourselves, but my nightly bath really is a much-needed part of my day. I think everyone should do it.

I know you may be thinking, *I don't have time for that! I have way too much to do, and I rarely get to sit still. I'm happy when I get a quick shower.* There is, and always will be, work to be done (as we will learn on Day 16 in "Manicure"). But there is also a time to rest; a time to soak. Psalm 46:10 says, "Be still, and know that I am God." Of course, by now you realize I'm talking not only about soaking our flesh but our spirit also—a spiritual soak. As believers we need to take time, each and every day, to soak in the presence of God, to hide away in the secret place.

BEAUTY INSIDER TIP 1

Jesus said one thing is needed

In Luke chapter 10, you can find the story of two sisters who each had a different relationship with Jesus. Mary, who took time to sit at the feet of Jesus, and Martha, who was distracted with serving. We can all relate to Martha; as women, there is a lot of serving to be done. We serve our husbands, children, houses, and so much more. There are endless chores to be done and bills to be paid—and that's only talking about our homes. We also serve in our local church, where there is always a job to do. Mary, unlike her sister, knew what was needed. She sat at Jesus' feet, resting in His presence.

The story goes on to tell us that Martha was distracted. After doing the cooking, serving, and cleaning, she became so frustrated with her sister's apparent laziness that she decided to approach Jesus with the matter, saying, "Lord, do You not care that my sister has left me to serve alone? Therefore tell her to help me" (v. 40). But Jesus answered with such love, "Martha, Martha, you are worried and troubled about many things. But one thing is needed, and Mary has chosen that good part, which will not be taken away from her" (vv. 41–42).

Often some, like Martha, think being busy for the Lord all the time is important to God. However, here Jesus is teaching us what is most important: sitting and soaking in His presence. He actually referred to it as "that good part." Psalm 46:10 says, "Be still, and know that I am God." Taking time to soak in the presence of the King is needed not only for Mary but for the whole body of Christ. Most of the time, we wake up with the best of intentions. We plan on spending quality time with the Lord. But because life is so busy, before we know it, the day has passed us by. We all need to be more like Mary and choose the good part.

* * *

One Father's Day weekend, my dad came to my house to visit; and I was excited about spending some time with him. We had just finished up with revival at church, and I had been very busy serving all weekend. My dad loves my cooking, so before I sat and visited with him, I wanted to run out to the store to get food for Father's Day dinner. He stopped me in my tracks. "Come here and sit down."

"I will as soon as I get back," I replied.

"I love your cooking," he said, "and it is so nice you want to do that for me, but I'd rather see you. Forget cooking. We'll go out to dinner."

I sat down with a sigh of relief and enjoyed my dad's company. He enjoyed that more than the finest feast I could have prepared. And so it is with our Lord.

All the service you give to the Lord will never replace the time He wants to spend with you. He appreciates all we're willing to do—but not at the cost of our one-on-one time with Him.

James 4:8 says, "Draw nigh to God, and he will draw nigh to you" (KJV). If it's been a long time since you've felt the closeness of His presence, maybe He's trying to stop you in your tracks. Can you hear Him saying, *Come and sit down for a while*?

BEAUTY INSIDER TIP 2

Soak away worry and get a good night's sleep

Soaking in a bath is as much about relaxing as it is cleansing. It's an opportunity to wash away not only dirt but worry also. Studies have shown that soaking in the tub every day for eight weeks can be more effective in relieving anxiety than a prescription drug. If a soak in the natural can accomplish that, imagine how much can be done through a spiritual soak. Taking time to bask in His presence becomes a time of exchange: we trade worry for peace, fear for faith, and sorrow for the joy of the Lord (Psalm 16:11). To give us "beauty for ashes, the oil of joy for mourning, the garment of praise for the spirit of heaviness" (Isaiah 61:3).

Another natural benefit to soaking is it relaxes the muscles. Having relaxed muscles helps us rest physically and mentally. In Psalm 84:10, the psalmist writes, "Better is one day in your courts than a thousand elsewhere" (NIV). No matter how stressed your day might have been, no matter what you may be facing, if you take time to spend in His courts, His presence will calm all your fears and anxieties. For all who struggle with a good night's sleep, it is believed that when you come out of a hot bath and slip between the cool sheets, a signal is sent to your brain, causing you to sleep well.

Again, we can liken this to soaking in the presence of God. By the time we are finished soaking in the Spirit, we should be able to drift off into a peaceful, sweet sleep.

BEAUTY INSIDER TIP 3

His presence prepares you

Once the hot water penetrates your tense muscles and the aroma from the bath bomb begins to ease your thoughts, your body and your mind will relax. All this, and you haven't done anything except sit and soak. When your mind becomes free from worry, you are now prepared to pray effectively. Fear and worry will hinder your faith and will make your prayer life unfruitful. By spending time with Him, you will be relieved of your burdens. In Matthew 11:28, Jesus gives an invitation: "Come to Me, all you who labor and are heavy laden, and I will give you rest."

Some people think of prayer as a task, as something they have to do. Yet prayer is a privilege; something we get to do. Do you feel that spending time with someone you love is difficult? No, it's a pleasure. Start to think about prayer as time spent visiting with someone you love and respect. Someone who loves you in return and has the answer to any problem you may have. It will change your whole attitude about your prayer time.

Prayer is not just us talking to God but also taking time to listen to Him. Effective prayer is not a monologue, where one person does all the talking, but a dialogue, where more than one person speaks. We should anticipate a response from God. We bring our praise, our worship, and our petitions before Him, and He will respond. When we think about prayer from this perspective, we will do a lot less talking and a lot more listening.

To the believer, prayer should become as natural as breathing. No one has to tell us to breathe. It should be enjoyable talking to the Lord about everything and remaining in constant fellowship with Him throughout our day. But prayer has to start somewhere. This is why the secret place is so important. When Jesus instructed His disciples how to pray (Matthew 6:6), He told them to go in and shut the door.

The purpose of the shut door is to shut out distractions. He said this because He knew how easily we can become distracted (like Martha). This doesn't mean we aren't to ever pray in public, but we have to understand the value of private prayer. Pray in private, and God will reward you openly. If we take time to shut the door, sit quietly, and hear Him, it will become easier to recognize His voice throughout our day.

Spending time in His presence also prepares us for the plan He has for our lives. Esther 2:12 talks about the preparation Esther went through in order to go before the king. This preparation took time and could not be rushed. She went through twelve months of soaking, scouring, and polishing. When she appeared before the king, she found favor in his sight. That favor was used to save her people. You never know what God is preparing you for while you're spending time with Him. Whatever it is, if you will faithfully take time in His presence, you will be ready for what lies ahead.

* * *

One morning, I was sitting in my prayer chair soaking in the presence of God. I was quietly praying in the Spirit when all of a sudden, a man in a runaway truck came crashing through the trees, the fence, and into my backyard. His truck stopped a few feet short of my pool. My time in the presence of God allowed me to stay calm and continue to pray as I ran to help the man, who was unconscious.

I tried to witness to him, but he was very confused and could barely hear me. As the ambulance whisked him away, I thought I would never see him again, but two months later a knock came to the door. It was Jack, the man who crashed in my yard. I told him in detail the story of his accident and how God had miraculously spared his life.

I believe that while I was soaking in the presence of God that day, He had me begin to pray in the Spirit and intercede for Jack. The Lord prepared me for what was about to happen. I told Jack the unbelievable course of events that landed him safely in my backyard could only be explained as the grace of God. I began to witness to him again. This time his mind was clear and his heart was overwhelmed by what God had spared him from. Jack couldn't remember anything about that morning—not the crash, my house, or even the paramedics. But he remembered one thing: me telling him about Jesus.

Because of my time spent soaking that morning, there was an undeniable presence of the Lord surrounding me. It was so powerful, the Spirit of the Lord was able to penetrate Jack's mind, even though he was in such a state of confusion. Right there on my back porch, Jack and I held hands and prayed as he received salvation.

Daily Reflection

Read Luke 10:38–42

- Which sister do you most identify with: Mary or Martha?

Read Proverbs 3:24

- What does this verse promise concerning rest?

Read Ephesians 2:10

- What could God be preparing you to do today?

Application

Soaking in the presence of God is an absolute necessity for a long-lasting relationship with Him. Remember the words of Jesus: one thing is needed. This one thing—sitting and soaking at the feet of Jesus—is needed for fellowship with Him and rest for you. And it benefits those around you, as we can see with Jack. There are so many other benefits from spending time with the Lord, but they could never fit into one book, much less a one-day study. You never know what spending time in His presence is preparing you for.

If you are willing to draw close to Him, He will draw close to you. Prepare, and—most importantly—make time. You might want to have a Bible, a notebook, or some worship music. Whatever you do, don't rush while you're soaking. Be patient in His presence; He's always patient with you.

DAY 3

Exfoliate

Mary Forrest

If anyone is in Christ, he is a new creation;
old things have passed away;
behold, all things have become new.

2 CORINTHIANS 5:17

Exfoliating is one of the many processes we go through to prepare our skin and to keep it looking its best. To exfoliate literally
means to remove the surface or to come apart. When we exfoliate our skin, we scrub with something rough to remove layers of
dead skin, oil, and dirt that have built up. What we have left is the
bright, clean, and shiny new surface that was hidden underneath.
Now it's been made ready or prepared for whatever process is
coming next.

Let's face it: Scrubbing off the flesh doesn't sound enjoyable, no matter how good the results will be. And yet even though crucifying, or getting rid of, the flesh is not fun, it's absolutely necessary. The apostle Paul explains this in Galatians 2:20: "I am crucified with Christ: nevertheless I live; yet not I, but Christ liveth in me" (KJV). Jesus Himself didn't want to face crucifixion, but the benefits of His obedience are endless, as are the benefits we receive by crucifying our flesh.

Some beauty processes are certainly more enjoyable than others. Yesterday's "Soak" was relaxing and refreshing. We need the soak to soften the skin. Think about when you get a manicure or pedicure. Before they start removing the dead skin, they soak it. Taking the time to soak in His presence will soften up our flesh and make it a lot easier to exfoliate. Exfoliating is for our own good. "He must increase, but I must decrease" (John 3:30).

BEAUTY INSIDER TIP 1

Exfoliating prevents breakouts

One of the greatest benefits of exfoliating is that it prevents breakouts. When dead skin cells build up on the surface of our skin, it clogs pores and causes acne. And who wouldn't want to prevent that? The first thing someone sees when they look at you is your face. I don't know of anyone who would choose to be seen with red, inflamed, bumpy skin. Sometimes we try to cover up these breakouts, which usually ends up making it appear worse instead of better.

As women of God, we ought to show a bright, healthy face that's gleaming for Jesus. But, if we're honest, we all sometimes show that we have not learned how to control our breakouts.

Maybe we show it in the way we speak or answer someone, or in our attitudes toward one another. Whatever it is that causes us to personally struggle, in Christ we don't have to find a way to cover up our ugly flesh. With His help, we can learn to keep our flesh under control. We can scrub away the dead things that need not be there, leaving us to be a witness to all those around.

One of the ways God helps us exfoliate is by using other people. Have you ever had someone that rubbed you the wrong way? Of course you have. All of us have people in our lives who irritate our flesh. We like to call her "Sister Sandpaper." You know who I'm talking about—it's as if she's on a mission to aggravate you. But no matter how much your flesh dislikes her, your spirit should love her, because she's helping you exfoliate.

BEAUTY INSIDER TIP 2

We can age gracefully

Allowing dead skin cells to build up on the surface of our skin will not only cause breakouts but also the appearance of fine lines and wrinkles. Some of us live in fear of wrinkles. Using anything from expensive creams to antiaging products to special beauty treatments, people everywhere are desperate to find a way to avoid aging (maturing). Just like with our natural skin, this is another reason that exfoliating our flesh will benefit us spiritually. When Christ returns for His church, He is coming to "present her ... as a radiant church, without stain or wrinkle or any other blemish" (Ephesians 5:27 NIV). Neglecting to put our flesh under subjection to the Holy Spirit and to His Word will cause wrinkles in our walk.

The quest to stay young is nothing new. In fact, it seems to have been a trend throughout history, dating back even to the sixteenth century with Spanish explorer Ponce De Leon searching for the fountain of youth. This fountain was supposedly a spring that was able to restore the youth of anyone who would drink from it or bathe in it. Some of us want to be young forever, but in 1 Corinthians 13:11, the apostle Paul talks about being a child and then becoming a man. What does that mean? It simply means aging is a part of life; it's inevitable. In the same way, we also come to a time in our relationship with the Lord when we must mature spiritually and put away childish things.

"But grow in the grace and knowledge of our Lord and Savior Jesus Christ" (2 Peter 3:18). To mature in the Lord, we have to radically change our priorities from living to please ourselves to living to please God and learning to obey Him. We do this by fasting, prayer, and spending time with Him in His Word. The good news is that we don't have to avoid aging. On the contrary, we need to embrace it, because when we exfoliate our flesh, we will begin to mature in Christ. Then, only through Him, we can be radiant and without wrinkles as He has always intended us to be.

"Let the beauty of the LORD our God be upon us" (Psalm 90:17). He will allow us to age gracefully as He renews us daily in the beautiful image in which He created us.

BEAUTY INSIDER TIP 3

It's all about maintenance

In order to receive any of its benefits, we need to exfoliate regularly. A little while after exfoliating, dead skin cells begin to build back up on our skin's surface. It isn't something we can do once and be done with. Jesus said in Luke 9:23, "If anyone desires to come after Me, let him deny himself, and take up his cross daily, and follow Me." The same principle applies to our inner beauty process. In 1 Corinthians 15:31, Paul speaks about dying daily to the flesh. Our flesh will always begin to build itself back up if we haven't taken time to regularly bring it under subjection to the Word.

Regularly exfoliating also helps to balance out your skin. Scripture says that the enemy is roaming around ready to devour at all times. "Be sober [well balanced and self-disciplined], be alert and cautious at all times. That enemy of yours, the devil, prowls around like a roaring lion [fiercely hungry], seeking someone to devour" (1 Peter 5:8 AMP). But the person who is well balanced and walking in the Spirit is not the easy prey he's looking for. Paul teaches us to "walk in the Spirit, and you shall not fulfill the lust of the flesh" (Galatians 5:16).

If you haven't exfoliated in a while, chances are your skin is dull, lackluster, and possibly broken out. As believers, that's not how we want to represent Christ. We need to spend regular time crucifying our flesh through fasting, prayer, and studying His Word, which is loaded with benefits that will transcend far above any beauty product out there. When we do, we will reflect the bright, radiant, well-balanced bride the Lord intended us to be.

Daily Reflection

Read Proverbs 27:17

- Who could the Lord be using in your life as an exfoliant?

Read Colossians 3:8-10, 12-14

- What can you put *off* today, in the effort to become spiritually mature?

- What can you put *on* today, in the effort to become spiritually mature?

Read Psalm 103:1-5

- What are some of the benefits of regular time spent with the Lord?

Application

Have you ever bought a new product to use on your skin, and you didn't feel like it did anything at all? Maybe it even made it look worse. Don't be quick to think it was the product that didn't deliver. The truth is, you cannot receive the full benefits of your beauty products if you haven't exfoliated first. The layers of dead skin that are in the way will make it impossible for anything that comes next to be effective.

We can't expect to receive all the benefits of a moisturizer when we haven't successfully learned to exfoliate. Likewise, we can't mature in our walk with the Lord until we've learned how to get ourselves out of His way. We will be radiant when our wants change into what He wants for us. "Bless the Lord, O my soul; ... and forget not all His benefits" (Psalm 103:1-2). He has so much waiting for us. More than we can even imagine, if we would just allow Him to lead us into removing all the dirt and dead things in our lives. He wants to transform us into inner beauties as we walk in His glorious image.

DAY 4

Moisturizer

Bessie Hicks

"If anyone thirsts, let him come to Me and drink. He who believes in Me, as the Scripture has said, out of his heart will flow rivers of living water." But this He spoke concerning the Spirit, whom those believing in Him would receive. The Holy Spirit was not yet given, because Jesus was not yet glorified."

JOHN 7:37–39

Have you ever allowed your skin to get really dry?

I recently took a trip to the beach. After spending all day in the saltwater, I was thirsty and my skin was so dry I thought it would crack. I couldn't wait to get back to the room for a bottle of water, a nice shower, and my moisturizer. A good moisturizer is like a glass of water to your thirsty skin—nothing feels better.

In the natural, it's your skin's best friend. In the spirit, the Holy Ghost is like our moisturizer; He's our best friend sent from God, to comfort us and quench our every thirst.

Living without the Holy Spirit's help is like trying to live without water. It makes you spiritually dehydrated. Dehydration, in the natural, creates all sorts of problems—one of them being exhaustion. If at any time you are feeling spiritually tired, worn down, or discouraged, perhaps you're dehydrated in the spirit and need a drink from the Holy Ghost. He is there to help you in every area. For those things that may wear you out in the natural and in the spirit, a dose of the Holy Ghost is your answer.

BEAUTY INSIDER TIP 1

The Holy Spirit is our helper

Have you ever heard the phrase *combination skin*? It requires a moisturizer that brings balance to even out your skin. You may have a combination of problems, but the Holy Spirit is always a perfect balance. He meets your personal needs because He is a person, the third person of the Trinity. There is God the Father, God the Son, and God the Holy Spirit, and all three of them are One!

"Nevertheless I tell you the truth. It is to your advantage that I go away; for if I do not go away, the Helper will not come to you; but if depart, I will send Him to you" (John 16:7). Jesus spoke these words to His disciples. It was to their advantage to have Jesus in heaven and the Holy Spirit on earth. Jesus had limited Himself (for our sake) by becoming a man, but the Holy Spirit would have no such limitations. He is all-knowing (omniscient), all-powerful (omnipotent), and present everywhere at once (omnipresent).

Let's take a look at some of the ways the Holy Spirit can help us.

- **Personal guide** (John 16:13): Have you ever been on a guided tour? The guide leads you and points out all the things you may not have noticed on your own. He knows the history, the mysteries, and everything in between. He knows what's around the corner before you even get there. The Holy Spirit was sent to guide us and show us things to come.

- **Personal teacher** (1 John 2:27): The Holy Spirit is our teacher. He's actually more like our tutor because He gives us the one-on-one teaching we need. He is the author of the Bible. Who better to teach the Word than the one who wrote it (2 Timothy 3:16)! Not only does He teach us the Scriptures; He can also teach us to do anything. I've heard testimonies of people who have learned to read, play instruments, even write books, all by way of the Spirit. He can teach us how to be a wife, a mother, a preacher, and anything else we need to know.

- **Prayer partner** (Romans 8:26): Have you ever been in a situation and don't know what to pray? The Holy Spirit is here to help us, especially when it comes to praying. He knows the mind of God and the will of God in every situation. He knows what to say and how to say it. If we will learn to rely on Him in prayer and let the Spirit pray through us, we will see the answers we so desperately need.

- **Personal search engine** (1 Corinthians 2:10): Do you remember what it was like before we had Google? Being able to search anything on the Internet with one click completely changed the way we live. The Holy Spirit searches the deep things of God and makes them understandable to us. He also searches our hearts for verses we have hidden and brings them out when we need them (Psalm 119:11).

- **Personal spokesman** (Matthew 10:19–20): Sometimes we can say the right thing the wrong way, and other times we might not know what to say. The Holy Spirit wants to help us speak. He will give us the right words to say at the right time—to our husbands; to our children; in our business; and to a lost, dying world.

- **Personal best friend** (Proverbs 18:24): The Holy Spirit wants to be our best friend, and what a friend He is! He's there for you whenever you need Him. He will help in every situation, listen to all your problems, and give you the best counsel. He will stick closer than a brother (or sister). He's always got your back!

God sent the Holy Spirit to the disciples and us to be our personal helper in everything we do—all for our advantage.

BEAUTY INSIDER TIP 2

The Spirit is within us and upon us

You might be thinking, *I have the Spirit living in me. Why doesn't He do that for me?*

You may have the Spirit living in you, but are you living in Him? Let me explain. After you become born again, the Holy Spirit comes to live in you. He changes you on the inside. If you want to see Him working on the outside of you, you need to be in Him. This is done by the baptism of the Spirit.

Jesus said, "If you love Me, keep My commandments. And I will pray the Father, and He will give you another Helper, that He may abide with you forever—the Spirit of truth, whom the world cannot receive, because it neither sees Him nor knows Him; but you know Him, for He dwells with you and will be in you" (John 14:15–17).

According to *Strong's Concordance*, to be baptized means "to submerge." To make this easier to understand, think about the difference between drinking a glass of water and jumping into a pool. They are both water, but one goes in your body, and the other your body goes in. One is on the inside; the other is on the outside. It's the same with the Holy Spirit. At salvation, He comes to live in you. At baptism, He comes upon you, like jumping into a pool. When a person has been submerged in a pool, it will be obvious to those around them because they are soaking wet.

When you are born again, you certainly receive the Holy Spirit. He comes to live in you, changing you from the inside. However, there is another experience available to every believer; it's called the baptism of the Holy Spirit. The Spirit comes upon you to give you power to be His witness and to minister to others. These are two separate experiences but the same Spirit. It has been said that at salvation, you get the Holy Spirit—but at the baptism of the Spirit, He gets *you*.

Compare these passages from the Gospel of John. In both, Jesus refers to the Spirit of God as water, but He uses two analogies—a well and a river.

- **The Spirit of God as a well** (salvation): "Jesus answered and said to her, 'Whoever drinks of this water will thirst again, but whoever drinks of the water I shall give him will never thirst. But the water I shall give him shall become in him a fountain of water springing up into everlasting life'" (4:13–14).

- **The Spirit of God as a river** (baptism of the Spirit): "Jesus stood and cried out, saying, 'If anyone thirsts, let him come to Me and drink. He who believes in Me, as the Scripture has said, out of his heart will flow rivers of living water.' But this He spoke concerning the Spirit" (7:37–39).

Although a well and a river both contain water, they are two different things. In John 7:37–39, Jesus begins to speak about being thirsty again. This time, He said that if you come to Him and drink, out of your belly will flow rivers of living water. Why did Jesus use a different picture/type of water this time? Because a river is active and flowing, bringing life wherever it goes (Ezekiel 47). The river Jesus is referring to is the baptism of the Holy Spirit, a river that will flow from the innermost part of you.

At the baptism of the Holy Spirit, you become so full of the Spirit, He begins to flow out of you (if you allow Him) onto everything around you. There is so much more to study on the baptism of the Spirit. We will discover the power that's available to us, through Him, on Day 14 in "Blow-Dry."

BEAUTY INSIDER TIP 3

The Holy Spirit pulls you up, not down

There is one very important rule to remember while applying moisturizer: Never pull down on your skin. If you continually pull down on your skin, wrinkles will eventually form. The correct way to apply moisturizer is a method that's been around for years, called "up and out." It's as simple as it sounds. Rather than pulling down, use a gentle motion moving upward, then outward.

The Holy Spirit pulls us up and out! If you're discouraged or down, He can lift you up. He's gentle like a dove and will not intrude on your situation. One of His most important jobs is mentioned in John 16:8: "He will convict the world of sin." With His gentle nature, He brings conviction in our lives by pointing out things that are displeasing to God. His correction is never for the purpose of condemnation or to make us feel bad. Instead, He reveals to us the area where we're falling short because He wants us to have the best life possible. He would never pull us down; He always lifts us up to encourage us.

Daily Reflection

Read Acts 2:1-4

- What was the initial evidence of Holy Spirit baptism?

Read Acts 10:44-46

- Who can receive the baptism of the Holy Spirit?

Read Acts 19:1-7

- Have you received the Holy Ghost since you believed?

Application

What would we do, or where would we be, without the Holy Spirit? From the beginning He has been at work in our hearts. At the time of salvation, He comes to live inside us and help us to live the Christian life. When we receive the baptism of the Spirit, He comes upon us and gives us the ability to minister to others with the same power Jesus had while He was here on earth.

If you desire a deeper personal relationship with the Holy Spirit and need Him to be your personal helper, then you need His baptism. Allow us to walk you through it. Turn to "Receiving the Baptism of the Holy Spirit" in the back of the book, which will lead you into receiving this gift. There is no reason to be scared, apprehensive, or intimidated. God is a good Father and desires to give you good gifts. Are you ready to receive them?

DAY 5

The Mask

Theresa Smith

"A good man out of the good treasure of his heart brings forth good; and an evil man out of the evil treasure of his heart brings forth evil. For out of the abundance of the heart his mouth speaks."

LUKE 6:45

We have soaked, cleansed, exfoliated, and moisturized in an attempt to keep our complexion healthy and clear. It seems that we women are constantly treating the surface of our skin. This is why it's so frustrating to still look in the mirror and see blemishes. I have learned that sometimes, to get the best results on the surface, I need to treat the underneath, hidden part of my skin. If my pores are not regularly treated, then dirt, oil, and dead skin will get trapped and can cause blemishes and wrinkles

44

on the surface. This is *not* what we want—so thank God for the beauty mask! With regular use, a deep-cleansing mask keeps my skin looking healthy, firm, and beautiful.

Just like our daily skin routine, we have to daily cleanse our hearts and minds. How? By spending time in His Word. The apostle Paul says that our Lord will be coming back for a church without spot, wrinkle, or blemish (Ephesians 5:27). Our Lord is so gracious that, through studying His Word, He shows us how to be ready for our Bridegroom.

As with our skin, we have to make time to treat the deeper issues—those of our heart. The Bible teaches that the words we say, and the things we do, flow from our heart. We must allow Him to clean the hidden parts of our hearts with the Word of God, to improve the surface. Like our skin, little things can build up in our hearts and start to show on the surface.

BEAUTY INSIDER TIP 1

Prevention and treatment

The best way to keep your skin clean is to catch the dirt, oil, and dead skin before blemishes form. But even those who take excellent care of their skin will occasionally require a deep cleansing. Therefore, we should use a mask weekly, biweekly, or monthly for preventive measures. And keeping a regular check on our hearts is even more important. After all, according to Romans 3:23, "all have sinned, and come short of the glory of God" (KJV).

Just as none of us are exempt from the occasional blemish on the skin, none of us are exempt from having allowed our hearts to become blemished. Psalm 51 is an account of David crying out to God to heal his blemished heart: "Have mercy upon me, O God, according to Your lovingkindness; … Blot out my transgressions. Wash me thoroughly from my iniquity" (vv. 1–2). He knew he had sin in his heart and admitted it before the Lord. He asked God not to just remove his iniquity but to cleanse his heart. "Create in me a clean heart, O God, and renew a steadfast spirit within me" (v. 10).

While a mask is mostly used to prevent breakouts, it can also be used as a treatment for them. If you are seeing blemishes on the surface, it is a sign of a problem underneath, and a deep cleansing is a must. In Psalm 139:23–24, David asked of the Lord, "Search me, O God, and know my heart; … see if there is any wicked way in me." What a perfect example of seeking God as a preventative measure. David prayed and asked God to show him if there was anything offensive he may be harboring. He was doing as Proverbs 4:23 teaches—guarding his heart.

BEAUTY INSIDER TIP 2

Do it for yourself

Applying a beauty mask is not something that you're going to do in front of others. Covering your face with wet, slimy stuff is something most of us would choose to do alone. But this is a good thing because sometimes, we women need to be alone. Asking God to cleanse our hearts is also something that requires privacy. It's an opportunity to be alone with God, without having to share the ugly with anyone else. He knows everything in our hearts anyway.

"O LORD, You have searched me and known me. You know my sitting down and my rising up; you understand my thought afar off" (Psalm 139:1–2).

BEAUTY INSIDER TIP 3

Follow the process

A mask will always work best if you follow the process.

First, it should always be applied on clean, moist skin. Invite the Holy Spirit to come and wet your heart with living water. He always needs to be present. Our minds cannot know what might be hidden in our hearts, we need the Spirit to reveal it. Paul writes in 1 Corinthians 2:10, "For the Spirit searches all things, yes, the deep things of God." When we seek and search God's Word, His alive and active Word, it will become like a mirror to our hearts.

Have you ever gotten dressed and thought you looked nice, but when you caught a glimpse of yourself in the mirror, you decided you needed to go change? The mirror revealed what you really looked like, not what you thought you looked like. This is what the Word does to our hearts. Paul referred to the Word of God in Hebrews 4:12 as a "discerner of the thoughts and intents of the heart."

Second, you have to get messy. This requires you to put your hands in the mud, goo, or whatever the mask is made of, and apply it liberally to your skin. In the same way, we need to dig into the Word of God and apply it generously to our hearts.

The third step is waiting. This is the one that we usually get bored with and sometimes become tempted to rush. But, like James 1:4 says, "let patience have its perfect work." The mask has to set and dry in order to draw out the impurities. We need to wait on the Lord and listen for His voice. He will speak. Things may get uglier before they get better, but hold on! Let the work be complete.

Finally, when it's time to take the mask off, apply a warm cloth to your face and gently remove. This will reveal your clean, glowing skin. After the Holy Spirit and the Word have revealed what is in your heart, confess your sins and allow the Lord to remove them.

Daily Reflection

Read Proverbs 4:23

- What do you think Scripture means by "keep your heart"?

Read James 4:8

- What promise can you stand on today, according to this verse?

Read Jeremiah 17:9–10

- If you allow the Lord to search your heart, what would He find?

Application

It is God's plan for us to allow Him to wash us clean and to be glowing, without spot, wrinkle, or blemish. He sent His Son, Jesus, for that very purpose. If the mask you are applying is for prevention, then pray, keeping your heart open and your ears listening. Stay in the Word and allow the Holy Spirit to stand guard. If you are applying the mask for the treatment of blemishes, search the Word for verses concerning your struggles. Learn everything He has to say about that subject. Let Him shine His light and remove what is not of Him and reveal the new, improved you.

WEEK 2

Makeup

DAY 6

Foundation

Bessie Hicks

For no other foundation can anyone lay
than that which is laid, which is Jesus Christ.

1 CORINTHIANS 3:11

Makeup professionals will tell you the most important part of your makeup routine should be your foundation. It is the bottom layer of makeup that all your other makeup is built upon. It evens out your skin tone and helps everything else you apply stay in place. You should know this: you are probably not going to get complimented on your foundation, as you would on your lipstick or eyeliner. There is just nothing flashy about it. As a matter of fact, if your foundation is done right, it won't be noticed at all; but without it, the rest of your makeup simply will not last.

Think about the foundation of a house. No one is impressed with it; most people don't even notice it. They will comment on the floors, the windows, or the fabulous kitchen, but you will never hear them comment on what a beautiful foundation it has. The foundation is completely overlooked. But without it, nothing else could stand—not a fireplace or a chandelier or any of the other pretty things. Often, people will notice the blessings in the life of a believer: the beautiful peace they walk in, their children who are serving the Lord, or the anointing on their lives. What they may not realize is none of it would be possible without the proper foundation in the Word of God. It may not look pretty, but it will allow everything beautiful to have a place to stand.

Just as applying a good foundation is the most important part of your makeup routine, having a proper foundation in the Word is the most important part of building a relationship with the Lord and living a blessed life. Can you build on something if the foundation is not right? Sure, you can, but it would never last. Now ask yourself this question: What foundation am I built upon?

BEAUTY INSIDER TIP 1

Jesus is the foundation, and we are the church

First Corinthians 3:11 makes it clear that Jesus is our foundation. He is the Rock—the Chief Cornerstone—and if we build our lives upon Him, we will not be shaken. His completed work on the cross is the foundation of our salvation. King David said, "I waited patiently for the LORD; and He inclined to me, and He heard my cry. He also brought me up ... out of the miry clay, and set my feet upon a rock, and established my steps" (Psalm 40:1–2).

I don't know where you were when Jesus found you; I can only speak for myself. I was in the miry clay of this world. As sad as it sounds, I loved the world: its music, movies, and fashions—everything about it. I had made myself fit right in, yet I knew in my heart it wasn't where I belonged. I still went to church, because that's what I was raised to do—but my heart was far from Him. One day, over twenty years ago now, I cried out to the Lord. He heard my cry and lifted me out of the mire of this world. He placed my feet upon the solid rock, and I have been firm-footed ever since. What a foundation Jesus has been to me!

When we allow God, the Master Builder, to do the constructing, it will last. He said that He would build a church that could stand: "You are Peter, and on this rock I will build My church, and the gates of Hades shall not prevail against it" (Matthew 16:18). When Jesus spoke this, Peter had just received the revelation from God that Jesus is the Christ, the Son of the living God (v. 16). The revelation of who Christ is would be the Rock that the church is built upon. The word *church* had never been mentioned in the Bible prior to this.

"Coming to Him as a living stone, rejected indeed by men, but chosen by God and precious, you also, as living stones, are being built up a spiritual house" (1 Peter 2:4–5). We're His children. And as Jesus is the Chief Cornerstone of the church, we are the living stones—chips off the old block. We're the building blocks that make up the church—not a building, but a body of believers. We who were not a people have now become God's people, chosen by Him, and we are precious to Him—so valuable that He paid a great price for us.

With Jesus as our foundation, we can stand through anything. No matter what the enemy brings our way to try to bring us down, he will not prevail: "No weapon formed against [us] shall prosper" (Isaiah 54:17).

BEAUTY INSIDER TIP 2

Match yourself with the foundation

Italy has a famous landmark, the Leaning Tower of Pisa. The tower is 179 feet tall and moves about half an inch each year. You would not think that shifting that tiny amount yearly would make that much of a difference, but now it is seventeen feet off the plumb line. As of now, the tower is still standing. Eventually, however, it will fall—it's inevitable. The name of the tower gives us a clue as to how it got off track. *Pisa* means "marshland." The tower was built on soft ground, and the foundation was only ten feet deep.

The farther down a foundation is dug, the higher the building can stand. If we dig deeper into the things of God—building on nothing but the solid rock truth of God's Word—we will stand straight and tall. But if we are not careful to line our lives up with the Word of God, we are in danger of a fall. The tower of Pisa is still standing today, but how long will it last? Imagine the damage that could happen if or when it falls over. First Corinthians 10 warns the reader of this very thing: "Let him who thinks he stands take heed lest he fall" (v. 12).

If we go back to our makeup analogy for a minute, there is something important when it comes to our foundation. It has to match our skin. Every woman knows what I'm talking about. When someone's foundation does not match her face, you can see a horrible foundation line. A color, or tone, that's just a slight bit off is obvious to everyone around. With makeup, we match the foundation to our skin—but in the Spirit, we have to match ourselves with the foundation, Jesus Christ. If we get off by a little, we could end up toppling right over.

BEAUTY INSIDER TIP 3

Build your house upon the Rock

Most people want the same things out of life: a career; a nice home; a good marriage; healthy, happy children; and peace when you lay your head down at night. There are many different ways you can go about building your life, but there are shortcuts you cannot afford to take if you want lasting results—results that last throughout eternity. Did you know that the foundation of a house is usually the most expensive part? The foundation God has laid for you, through Jesus Christ, was very costly. I cannot imagine why anyone would want to build on something other than the best.

So many times, Christians go to church and hear the Word of God. They think to themselves, *That was so good*; then they leave the service and never actually become a doer of what they have just heard. When you're a hearer only, and not a doer of the Word, you're lying to yourself. James 1:22 says it like this: "Be doers of the word, and not hearers only, deceiving yourselves." We have a hard-enough time trying to combat the lies of the enemy, so why would we want to create further problems by lying to ourselves? That would be foolish! A wise man, however, builds his house upon the Rock.

Jesus told His disciples, "Whoever hears these sayings of Mine, and does them, I will liken him to a wise man who built his house on the rock: and the rain descended, the floods came, and the winds blew and beat on that house; and it did not fall, for it was founded on the rock" (Matthew 7:24-25). As a doer of the Word, you are strong and cannot be shaken. Your house is now built upon the Rock, and you have a sure foundation. When the storms come—because storms *will* come—you will be like the house that Matthew 7:25 describes.

At first glance, this parable about the wise man and the foolish man would make you think these two men were totally different. However, if you take another look, you can see they're alike in many ways. Here are some of their similarities: they were both building houses, they both heard the same instructions (divine truth), and they both faced a terrible storm. The outside of their houses was probably very similar. However, there was one thing that made the difference when it came time to stand— the foundation.

Up till now, we have made the point over and over that we must have a proper foundation. So how do we build our house (marriage; children; ministry; life) upon the Rock? By living our life according to the Word of God. Hearing His words alone does not make your foundation. You must hear His words and do them!

Daily Reflection

Read Isaiah 28:16

- Who do you believe is the Cornerstone?

Read 1 Corinthians 10:12

- What is the best way to avoid falling in your walk with the Lord?

Read Matthew 7:24–25

- What does Jesus call a person who builds his house on the Rock?

Application

When you find yourself falling short, or your life starting to fall apart, go back to the question you asked yourself at the beginning of today's study: What foundation am I built upon? You may be relying on yourself, or someone else, instead of building on the Word of God. He is your firm foundation, and if you hear His words, and do them, you will not fall. If there's an area of your life that feels shaky, go back to the Word. Allow the Lord to show you a verse for your situation and *apply* it. Quote the Word, meditate on the Word, and—most importantly—be a *doer* of the Word.

Blush

Bessie Hicks & Jenny Belle Stanley

*We have known and believed the love that God has for us.
God is love, and he who abides in love abides in God,
and God in him. ... We love Him because He first loved us.*

1 JOHN 4:16, 19

Going to a makeup counter can be overwhelming. There are so many choices. Some women like to use everything and can't get enough, while others choose to stick with a few basic items. Either way, you probably won't find a makeup bag that does not contain a blush. For me, it's a staple—an absolute must-have to bring color to my face. Blush actually makes me look healthier. Without it, I look lifeless. Since Jesus is our foundation, then His love for us would have to be our blush.

The central theme of the Bible is God's love for humankind—and even better, His love for me personally. Every Christian knows John 3:16. If you were raised in church, you are taught to memorize it as a child, so it would be imbedded in your heart. Ask any believer to quote a passage of Scripture, and most of the time this is what they will say, "For God so loved the world that He gave His only begotten Son, that whosoever believes in Him shall not perish but have everlasting life" (John 3:16).

Paul echoes this in Romans 5:8 when he wrote, "God shows his love for us in that while we were still sinners, Christ died for us" (ESV). And there isn't a famous quote about love to compare with his words in chapter 8:

> Yet in all these things we are more
> than conquerors through Him who
> loved us. For I am persuaded that
> neither death nor life, nor angels nor
> principalities nor powers, nor things
> present nor things to come, nor height
> nor depth, nor any other created thing,
> shall be able to separate us from the
> love of God which is in Christ Jesus our
> Lord. (vv. 37–39)

Have you ever experienced a public display of affection so overwhelming that you didn't know how to react? You actually begin to blush with the emotion of it. Well, there has never been a display of love that can compare to what Jesus has done for you. First John 3:1 says, "See what great love the Father has lavished on us" (NIV). The word *lavish* means to bestow something in generous amounts. It also means costly, splendid, luxurious, and expensive. God's love for us is all that and more. It never runs out or wears out. There is nothing we can do to change it. The very thought of His unconditional love would make anyone blush.

So how could we doubt His love for us when He has made such a display of it? Unfortunately, all too often, we find ourselves wondering, *How can He love me?* Usually this happens because the understanding of love we have is conditional: If we act this way or look that way, then we will be loved. But God's love is unconditional. It's not based upon our goodness or on what we have done; it's about His goodness and what *He* has done.

BEAUTY INSIDER TIP 1

His love is greater
than you could ever know

One of the benefits of wearing blush is using it to change the appearance of your face. Some women have a rounder face; and blush, when applied properly, can lengthen the shape. Other women have a longer face and need their blush to create an illusion of fullness. Whatever the need—width, length, depth, or height—blush can change it. Now think about that principle and apply it to God's love. Whatever the need—width, length, depth, or height—His love can change it. The Lord's love for us is limitless; it knows no boundaries. God has gone (and will go) to every height, width, and depth to prove His love for us. Understanding His love changes everything!

"That you, being rooted and grounded in love, may be able to comprehend with all the saints what is the width and length and depth and height—to know the love of Christ which passes knowledge" (Ephesians 3:17–19)—Paul's prayer for the church echoes in my heart as I write this study. I pray that you too would be able to know and comprehend a love that surpasses knowledge. As a teacher, my job is to explain the truth. Preachers proclaim the gospel, while teachers explain it. Yet, how could you explain the unexplainable or describe the indescribable love of God?

Words fall short; analogies just don't cut it; there's not a story that could do it. I know because I searched, starting with my heart. I thought of every book I had ever read; every story I had ever heard; every message I had ever preached. Then I searched the Internet looking for something that could help me teach you about the greatness of His love; something that could sum it all up. Although there was plenty of material I could have used, nothing seemed sufficient. That's when I realized no one can say it like God does in the Bible—the greatest love story ever told. The cross is the ultimate example, and nothing shows His love more clearly.

BEAUTY INSIDER TIP 2

Love is the highlight

Most women know that blush is for highlighting your cheekbones. High cheekbones have always been recognized as a feature of beauty. Unfortunately, not everyone is born with perfect cheekbones. Some of us could use a little highlight. This is where blush comes in. Most cosmetics are meant to blend in; you're not supposed to notice cover-up, foundation, or powder. Blush is different: It's supposed to be noticed. It's meant to draw attention to the area being highlighted.

For a moment, think about when you are studying your Bible. You highlight verses that are most important and you want to remember, to make them stand out—just like applying blush to your cheekbones to draw attention to them and make them stand out. Wouldn't it be nice if someone gave you highlights when you begin to study the Word of God? Learning to walk in His ways can seem overwhelming at the beginning. Highlights would let you know what is the most important, or what you should be doing first. That is exactly what Jesus does in Matthew 22:37–39: "'You shall love the LORD your God with all your heart, with all your soul, and with all your mind.' This is the first and greatest commandment. And the second is like it: 'You shall love your neighbor as yourself.'"

In a few short moments, Jesus summed up the entire Old Testament, thousands of years of history, and countless pages of theology with one word: *love*. God's love is the highlight of His Word, His work, and His world. It's the thing He wants to draw your attention to: God is love! The original Greek word for "love" in that verse is *agape*. Agape is God's kind of love. It's unconditional and not a feeling but a choice. This kind of love is impossible if God is not the source. We have to first receive His love before we can ever give it to anyone else. Jesus also said in Matthew, "Freely you have received, [now] freely give" (10:8).

I once heard an explanation of how love works, using the cross as a model:

The first part of the cross is the part that goes vertical (up and down). It represents God's love for us. This is like our relationship with God. We receive His love from above and return it back to Him.

The second part of the cross runs horizontal (side to side). It represents our love for one another.

It's impossible to hang the second piece on the cross (our love for each other) when the first piece (our love for God) isn't in place. There would be nothing there to hang it on. Our love for one another is held up by our love for God. "By this shall all men know that ye are my disciples, if ye have love one to another" (John 13:35 KJV).

BEAUTY INSIDER TIP 3

Perfect love casts out fear

Throughout this study we have talked about blush bringing life and color to our faces. Well, fear does the exact opposite. Have you ever seen someone who is full of fear? It is written all over their face. You know the expression "white as a sheet"? Medically speaking, fear and anxiety can actually cause the color to drain from your face, leaving you looking lifeless. The good news is that perfect love is the antidote for fear. A revelation of how much God loves you and how perfect His love is for you will chase fear away. "There is no fear in love; but perfect love casts out fear, because fear involves torment. But he who fears has not been made perfect in love" (1 John 4:18). This verse makes it clear—fear brings torment. However, you must keep in mind that there are several different kinds of fear. For instance, Proverbs 9 speaks about the reverential fear of God, that's described as the beginning of wisdom. We can also have rational fears that help us be cautious, like the fear a parent would have if they saw a car coming toward their toddler. But the fear that comes from the enemy brings torment.

Most of us have experienced the torment that comes through that kind of fear. But did you know that God wants us to be fearless in Him? We are commanded not to fear—365 times in the Bible. That would equate to one command covering each day of the year! That doesn't mean we will never experience the feelings of fear, but we must recognize that God is not the source of fear. Rather, fear is an attack from the enemy. We need to receive what God has given us—love—rather than what the enemy wants to give us (fear), "for God has not given us a spirit of fear, but of power and of love and of a sound mind" (2 Timothy 1:7).

I like the following description of fear:

False
Evidence
Appearing
Real

And it is this kind of fear that God wants us to challenge and overcome.

I understand that receiving power, love, and a sound mind, rather than entertaining fear, is easier said than done. There is a common description for fear that may remind you to stand on the Word of God when you are feeling fearful. Sometimes the evidence that we are faced with appears more real than the truth of God's Word. Believing the promises of God becomes difficult when everything we see appears to be the opposite. That's when our faith is put to the test and when we must trust that He loves us.

Matthew 14:22–30 shows us an example of how fear can overtake us if we don't keep our eyes on Jesus. Jesus sent His disciples in a boat to the other side of the sea. You can imagine their fear when a storm arose and the waves began to toss them about. In the middle of the night, Jesus came walking to them on the sea, and they thought He was a ghost. In the natural, they had every reason to be fearful; but Jesus said to them, "Be of good cheer! It is I; do not be afraid" (v. 27).

When Peter realized it was Jesus, he was no longer afraid. He was brave. The very presence of Jesus calmed him. When perfect love showed up, fear was cast out. Instead of being afraid for his life, Peter was walking on the water with Jesus. When we realize how perfect His love is for us, our fears will disappear, because we know He always shows up.

Daily Reflection

Read Romans 8:35

- What can separate us from the love of Christ?

Read 1 Corinthians 13:4-8, 13

- Which of the sixteen discriptions of love do you find the easiest to exercise, and which are the most difficult?

Read Matthew 14:30

- What caused Peter to sink?

Application

When you think about applying blush, of course your mind goes to your cheeks. But when I (and most of the women I know) apply it, I start with the apple of my cheeks and work my way up. Then I put some down the bridge of my nose; next, a bit on my chin; and finally, a swipe on my forehead. In ancient times, they even used blush for lipstick; and it can double as eyeshadow. Basically, you can put blush just about anywhere. Love is the same way: "And above all things have fervent love for one another, for 'love will cover a multitude of sins'" (1 Peter 4:8).

DAY 8

Eyeliner

Theresa Smith

The eyes of your understanding being enlightened;
that you may know what is the hope of His calling,
what are the riches of the glory of His inheritance in the saints.

EPHESIANS 1:18

If I had to choose one piece of makeup, it would definitely be eyeliner. To me, it makes the most difference in changing, or completing, a look. Without it, makeup just doesn't look right. Of course, to achieve the best look, you need it all—mascara, lipstick, and more. But eyeliner makes your eyes pop, changing your whole look. When applied correctly, eyeliner will make your eyes appear to be more open as well as highlight the beauty that is already in your eyes. For example, plum-colored eyeliner accents the golden flecks in the eyes. The gold color is already there, but you may not notice it unless you apply the eyeliner.

When we want a different look, we sometimes line our eyes to change our natural apperance, but God wants to change our spiritual look. He wants us to see what He sees and to show us what we cannot see with eyes that haven't been enlightened.

BEAUTY INSIDER TIP 1

We are enlightened

Second Kings 6 tells the story of a servant who needed a different look. Elisha, a prophet, had been warning God's people of their enemies' locations. When the Syrian army found out that Elisha had been spoiling their attack plan, they sought to capture him. The Syrians sent an army with chariots and horses to surround the city where Elisha was. Elisha's servant arose in the morning to see an army surrounding them, and he was so afraid.

But Elisha was calm and collected. He told his servant, "Do not fear, for those who are with us are more than those that are with them" (v. 16). Then he prayed, "Open his eyes that he may see" (v. 17). The Lord opened the servant's eyes so he could see the mighty army of the Lord with horses and chariots of fire lined around him. The Lord had the army there all along—but until the servant's eyes were open and he was enlightened by the Lord, he wasn't able to see them.

Oh Lord, give us eyes to see what you see!

In Ephesians 1:17–18, Paul tells God's people he's praying for them to see differently, "that the God of our Lord Jesus Christ, the Father of glory, may give to you the spirit of wisdom and revelation in the knowledge of Him, the eyes of your understanding being enlightened." The definition of *enlightened* here, from *Strong's Concordance*, is "to bring light, render evident." In other words, he prayed that God would draw their attention to something that is there.

Just as we use eyeliner to enlighten our eyes and make them more noticeable in the natural, we need to bring light to our spiritual eyes so we can be aware of what is there in Christ.

BEAUTY INSIDER TIP 2

We have hope in Christ

In verse 18 of Ephesians 1, Paul also prayed that believers would "know what is the hope of His calling." *Strong's Concordance* defines *hope* as the expectation of good. It defines *calling* as an invitation to a feast or to embrace the salvation of God.

Imagine being invited to a royal wedding! It will be the greatest feast of all time. You would plan the perfect gown, hair, and makeup for months. It would be all you could think about, with the expectation of what you will see. Well, guess what: God is inviting us to His feast—the wedding of all weddings. As the bride of Christ, we can expect great things from this invitation! As we prepare ourselves for this wedding, we will have hope of good things to come, from now into eternity.

To some people, the word *hope* can mean "iffy." They may "hope" for something, but not actually have confidence that it will come to pass. But the Word says in Romans 5:5, "Hope does not disappoint." We can be sure our hope in Christ will not let us down. No disappointment here. When God promises, He delivers. Paul longed for believers to know "the riches of the glory of His inheritance in the saints, and what is the exceeding greatness of His power toward us who believe, according to the working of His mighty power" (Ephesians 1:18–19). Also in his letter to the Ephesians, Paul cites God's grace as one of the purposes of his ministry to "preach among the Gentiles the unsearchable riches of Christ" (3:8).

Earlier, in verses 3–5, he writes about revelation. He says God has revealed to His people, by the Holy Spirit, the mystery of Christ. As "fellow heirs, of the same body, and partakers of His promise in Christ" (v. 6), we are part of the same body. When our earthly family (our flesh and blood) passes away, they leave us an inheritance of whatever riches they may have had. We don't receive this inheritance because we have earned it; we receive our earthly inheritance because of whose we are, or who we belong to. The same goes for the unsearchable riches of Christ we receive because we belong to Him. What belongs to Christ also belongs to us—and all our hope should be in Him. He has opened our eyes and revealed this to us, by the revelation of the Holy Spirit. Praise be to God!

BEAUTY INSIDER TIP 3

We've got the power!

We have access to all of God's power and promises. All throughout God's Word, we see He has given us His power.

In Acts 1:8, Jesus says, "You shall receive power when the Holy Spirit has come upon you; and you shall be witnesses to Me in Jerusalem, and in all Judea and Samaria, and to the end of the earth." This verse says we receive power after the Holy Spirit comes upon us, and we will become witnesses—people who see or hear something and can retell it.

If you read Romans 8:11, you will find out that His Spirit gives us resurrection power. The very same Spirit that raised Christ from the dead lives in us. The apostle Paul understood that this power will do us no good without revelation of who it comes from and why He gave it. He prayed that we would comprehend the greatest treasure we could ever receive. Ephesians 3 closes with, "Now to Him who is able to do exceedingly abundantly above all that we ask or think, according to the power that works in us, to Him be glory in the church by Christ Jesus to all generations, forever and ever. Amen" (vv. 20–21).

This power given to us by the Holy Spirit is not only helpful in our daily lives but is essential for ministry. The Holy Spirit gives us the power to see and hear the things of God and retell them—for His glory.

Daily Reflection

Read Ephesians 1:15-19

- What two things does Paul pray for the believer to receive?

Read Romans 4:18

- What did Abraham have hope in?

Read Ephesians chapter 3

- What do you think Paul was provoking the reader to know?

Application

We absolutely need our spiritual eyes opened; beauty is much more than skin deep. As eyeliner enlightens and shows off the hidden beauty of the eyes, allow the Lord to open the eyes of your understanding. His enlightenment will show off the hope, riches, and power He has for those who love Him.

DAY 9

Lashes

Betty Lovell

Surely He has borne our griefs and carried our sorrows;
yet we esteemed Him stricken, smitten by God, and afflicted.
But He was wounded for our transgressions, He was bruised for
our iniquities; the chastisement for our peace was upon Him,
and by His stripes we are healed.

ISAIAH 53:4–5

What do the words *full* and *finished* bring to mind when related to makeup? Eyelashes of course. We all want full, finished lashes. You know, like the kind in the mascara commercials. The model bats her eyes, and it appears as if her lashes are resting on her cheeks. Lashes are usually the last touch when applying makeup.

Whatever brand of mascara we are using, it is always fullness we are looking for to finish our look.

As we move along in our study of the Word, I would like to look at one of the magnificent things our Savior desires for us to have. Just as a good father wants only the best for his children, our heavenly Father only wants the best for us. He has given us the ability to walk in the fullness of life that Jesus died for us to have. He desires for us to receive all He has accomplished by His finished work on Calvary.

BEAUTY INSIDER TIP 1

There's a purpose for lashes

Everything God created has a purpose. As beautiful as your lashes are, they aren't there just to emphasize your eyes and make you look better (although that is an added bonus). They are actually very sensitive and meant for your protection. When you blink (act), they bat away anything that may be harmful to your eyes, like dust and debris.

Just as our eyelashes serve a purpose, so did the lashes our Savior bore. After Pilate ordered for Jesus to be scourged (beaten or lashed), "he delivered Him to be crucified" (Matthew 27:26). This scourging created lashes or stripes on His back. Why would He subject Himself to such pain? The answer is simple: It was all for us! The purpose of the scourging was for our health and our healing. His desire is for His children to walk in divine health here on earth. If it were not so, He could have skipped over the lashing and gone straight to the crucifixion.

Even though we have lashes to protect our eyes, every once in a while something that doesn't belong tends to get in, which can be irritating and sometimes painful. Our first reaction is to rub or have someone blow into our eye. Sometimes we are even willing to put our fingers in our eyes to remove it. In other words, we try everything we can to handle the problem ourselves. Did you know the best thing to do is allow your eye to tear up? The water (tears) will form, washing it out and cleaning away the particles that have made their way through your lashes. The same principle applies in the spirit.

Psalm 107:20 tells us, "He sent His word and healed them." The Gospel of John declares that Jesus was the Word made flesh (1:14). And Paul encouraged husbands to love their wives, "just as Christ also loved the church ... that He might sanctify and cleanse her with the washing of water by the word" (Ephesians 5:26). One of the definitions for the word *cleanse* is to disinfect. Washing in the water of the Word will disinfect and take away infection or anything else that causes sickness, bringing healing and health to our flesh.

BEAUTY INSIDER TIP 2

He wants you to have fullness

When you're not feeling well, you aren't living in abundance or the fullness of life He died for you to have. The smallest thing, like a stuffy nose, can make you feel like your head may pop, making it hard to focus. The same is true when you have a fever with chills and you're freezing even though it may be 80 degrees outside. Let's face it: Chills or a head cold are really minor when we think of sickness. But God doesn't even want you to suffer with them, let alone a life-threatening illness. If you were to go to a doctor with any of these complaints, he would take out a tablet and write you a prescription. It would include your recommended treatment for healing, along with instructions. Once you fill your prescription and follow the doctor's orders, you start to feel better.

I am grateful for doctors, but did you know that Jesus is our Great Physician? He has written and filled our prescription for healing, and all we need to do is follow the Doctor's instruction. On the Lord's prescription tablet, you will find all the remedy and medicine needed for health and wholeness. Proverbs 7:1-3 says, "My son, keep my words, and treasure my commands within you. Keep my commands and live, and my law as the apple of your eye. Bind them on your fingers; write them on the tablet of your heart." Proverbs 4:20-22 gives similar advice: "My son, give attention to my words; incline your ear to my sayings. Do not let them depart from your eyes; keep them in the midst of your heart; for they are life to those who find them, and health to all their flesh."

Don't miss what these two proverbs are saying: One says to write God's Word on the tablet of your heart; the other tells you God's words are life and health. Following His instructions will lead you into an abundant, full life.

BEAUTY INSIDER TIP 3

Application requires reflection

We can't apply mascara without using a mirror to see our reflection. The mirror makes it possible to see where to apply the makeup, which will enhance (intensify, increase, or further improve the quality, value, or extent of) our eyes. Why would we think we can live an enhanced, abundant life without the Word of God reflecting our hearts and what we need to apply spiritually?

Reflection is the key to application in the book of James. He compares the Word of God to a mirror:

> But be doers of the word, and not hearers only, deceiving yourselves. For if anyone is a hearer of the word and not a doer, he is like a man observing his natural face in a mirror; for he observes himself, goes away, and immediately forgets what kind of man he was. But he who looks into the perfect law of liberty and continues in it, and is not a forgetful hearer but a doer of the work, this one will be blessed in what he does. (1:22–25)

The Word is our spiritual mirror to look into and see what needs to be applied and where to apply it. In His mirror, I see health, healing, and wholeness. As you begin to reflect (meditate on; ponder) in His mirror, your faith for divine health will also increase. By reading, studying, hearing, and applying the verses on healing, you will also see health, healing, and wholeness. The Word tells us in Romans 10:17, "Faith comes by hearing, and hearing by the word of God."

In the New Testament, there are countless people who were healed. Jesus did not deny a single person who came to Him for healing. Whether it was a simple fever, a lame man walking, the deaf hearing, or the blind seeing, when the Word (Jesus) spoke, sickness had to go. The Word says in Matthew 9:35, "Jesus went about all the cities and villages, teaching in their synagogues, preaching the gospel of the kingdom, and healing every sickness and every disease among the people."

Some that came to Him for healing had a part to play, but when they acted on what He said, they were healed. Faith produces action. Here are just a few of the things that faith in, and obedience to, the words Jesus spoke caused people to do: rip a roof off a house; wash in a pool; ask; reach out and touch the hem of His garment; cry out; take up a bed and walk; and come forth.

In Matthew 9, the woman with the issue of blood said, "If I only may touch His garment, I shall be made well" (v. 21). She pressed through the crowd to reach out and touch the hem of His garment. Do you see what Scripture is teaching? True faith is followed by actions. Our words, like this woman's, should also line up with the truth of God's Word. This woman could have made an excuse by saying, "I'm considered unclean and I'm not supposed to be out in public." Likewise, the lame man in John 5 could have made his excuses, saying he was lame, when told to take up his bed and walk. There was also a leper in Luke 17 who, when instructed to show himself to the priest, could have said, "I'm not allowed to go through town or in the temple."

The truth is, each of these people had valid excuses not to do what they were instructed, but each one had faith to go against the grain. Actually, that is all Jesus asked for. Faith the size of a mustard seed—just a little tiny grain of faith—can move mountains! The Word is alive and living (Hebrews 4:12), with the ability to produce and bring forth time and time again. If we allow the Word to take root in our hearts, it will produce.

Go back and read the passage we opened with, Isaiah 53. Notice the use of the word *our*. Everything our Savior went through was for our benefit. He endured our punishment so we don't have to. *Our* is used five times in this one portion of Scripture. All the things we equate with sickness, Jesus took (bore) for us. The last thing He endured on this earth before He went to the cross was the scourging at the pillar. Without it, our health and our healing would not be complete.

Sometimes prolonged sickness can make us tired and weary, creating a change in our personality. Someone who had once been happy and bubbly may now seem to be sad or bitter. But God even made provision for that. Because of His lashes, we no longer have to be filled with grief and sorrow or be stricken and smitten, afflicted or wounded, bruised or chastised. We get to walk in health, healing, and fullness of life.

Daily Reflection

Read Acts 10:38

- Who is the oppresser, and what did Jesus come to do?

Read John 10:10

- Why did Jesus come?

Read Isaiah 53:4-5 and 1 Peter 2:24

- Can you spot the difference between these two passages?

Application

The passages in 1 Peter and Isaiah 53 may at first appear to be the same, but one word is different: *were*. By His stripes, we *were* healed. Peter wrote this after the lashes Jesus bore and after the crucifixion. He understood that our healing was finished at the cross and that we are now able to walk in the fullness of life He died for us to have. The next time you are finishing your makeup and applying your lashes, take a minute and reflect upon this: You were healed.

DAY 10

Lipstick

Becky Wharton

Because Your lovingkindness is better than life,
my lips shall praise You.

PSALM 63:3

Lipstick is the most-used cosmetic in a woman's makeup bag. Though few women carry around an entire case of makeup, most have at least one lipstick in their purse. Maybe it is so loved because it brightens our whole face. It protects, moisturizes, and (with just a little color) accentuates your lips—making what is already beautiful stand out. It is not intended to cover anything up but to make what is already there shine.

We have another kind of application for our lips. The Bible calls it praise. In Psalm 34:1, David wrote, "I will extol the LORD at all times; his praise will always be on my lips" (NIV). When we have praise on our lips, it protects, just like lipstick does, but not from the sun or from drying out. This spiritual lipstick of praise protects us from our enemy.

Recently, I heard a story about a young boy who ran the enemy out of his life through praising God. This ten-year-old was kidnapped from his own front yard in Atlanta, Georgia. The kidnapper threw him into the car and demanded that he not say a word. The boy began to sing praises to God. Over and over he praised, refusing to stay silent. After three hours of driving him around, the kidnapper couldn't listen to him praise another minute. He had to get away from his praising, so he pulled the car over and let out the boy, who returned home safely. The story was so amazing it made national news. Praising God in the darkest hour is still setting the captive free!

God wants your praise. Give him divine worship, especially when you're in a dark place in your life. Praise will give you strength. Nehemiah 8:10 says, "The joy of the Lord is your strength." Praise helps us look at God instead of our circumstances. We should wear praise on our lips like lipstick, carrying it around and reapplying it throughout the day. It is not difficult to praise Him if you look back on everything God has brought you through. With everything He has done for us, we always have a reason to praise our God.

BEAUTY INSIDER TIP 1

Praise brings protection

There is a story in 2 Chronicles 20 where praise protected God's people by confusing the enemy. King Jehoshaphat heard instruction from the Lord that his army was not supposed to fight in this battle. They were to "stand still and see the salvation of the LORD" (v. 17). Instead of natural weapons, he appointed singers to sing praises to the Lord on the front line (v. 21). As those appointed began to sing and praise, the Lord set an ambush against the armies of Ammon, Moab, and Mount Sier—all the armies who had come against Judah. By their obedience to sing and to praise, the enemy was defeated.

I was eighteen years old when my mom was diagnosed with Stage III cancer. I was devastated. I felt fear just like Jehoshaphat did. But I knew I could not stay in that frame of mind. I had to be strong for my mom and family. As the only daughter, I knew it was up to me to take care of my mom. Like Jehoshaphat, I started fasting and seeking the Lord. He was my only peace and comfort. I felt as if the Lord put an invisible bubble around me. Even though I heard the report of modern medicine, I kept my eyes focused on God and allowed Him to be my comfort. As I began to fast, pray, and give praises to Him, I became strong! I knew everything would be okay.

This battle was not mine, but God's (v. 15). I trusted Him and put the situation in His hands. God reminded me of how He sent His Son, Jesus, two thousand years ago to pay the price for healing with the lashes He bore. I stood firm in faith, reapplying my lipstick (praise) as needed, and I am here today to say my mom is almost eighteen years cancer-free. God has never left me. He has been so good to me and my family. I want to encourage you today to never let the enemy rob your praise. Worshiping God, even while in the battle, will defeat the enemy every time.

BEAUTY INSIDER TIP 2

Praise brings freedom

When applying lipstick, experts suggest you start in the center and work your way out. This allows your hand to become less shaky by the time you reach the outside of your lips. Praise also begins in the center, inside your heart, but it doesn't stay there; it has to work its way out. Just thinking about the goodness of God may be worship, but it's not praise. If you are going to praise God, it must be seen or heard. The good news is that the more you praise Him, the less shaky you become. Declaring the greatness of God usually starts with singing and rejoicing—and before you know it, the whole atmosphere is changed.

That's exactly what happened to Paul and Silas in Acts 16. They had been thrown into prison for preaching the gospel and praying for a young girl to be delivered. They were beaten and put into stocks, with a guard to make sure they stayed bound. Rather than complaining, they turned their prison sentence into a praise session. At midnight, they began to pray and sing praises to God—and they weren't quiet about it either. Their praise wasn't just in their heart; it was on their lips. While Paul and Silas were praising, the other prisoners listened. As they lifted their voices to God, suddenly God sent an earthquake—but they weren't shaken one bit. Verse 26 says, "All the doors were opened and everyone's chains were loosed."

Your praise doesn't just affect you; it will affect those around you. Many of us have loved ones who are bound. If we're not careful, we can become entangled by their bondage. It can become all we think about and could affect our peace; our relationships; our finances—every area of our life. It doesn't even have to be a substance addiction; some people are more bound by hatred or pride than anything else. Whatever the addiction may be, it affects everyone around them, creating an atmosphere of strife and confusion.

The good news is that praise can affect those around you. It also changes the atmosphere. When you begin to praise, God's presence is manifest. He said He inhabits the praises of His people (Psalm 22:3). David wrote in Psalm 18:3, "I will call upon the LORD, who is worthy to be praised; so shall I be saved from my enemies." The enemy can't stand praise, so if you're looking to run him out of your home and out of your life, praise is the way to do it.

BEAUTY INSIDER TIP 3

Praise builds confidence

In my brief study on lipstick, I found several opinions about the benefits of lipstick. The one thing every article had in common is this: wearing lipstick makes you feel more confident. My spiritual lipstick—praise—certainly builds my confidence. Not in myself but in my faith in God. As I recall all the things God has done in the past, the times He has come through, again and again, on my behalf, my heart begins to leap. Praising Him for past victories builds hope for future battles.

Sometimes we limit praise to the fast song during Sunday morning worship service, but praise is so much more. Opening your mouth and declaring the greatness of our God and giving Him glory is praising. We can do this by commending Him (directing our praise to Him and telling Him how wonderful He is). We can also praise Him by recommending Him (telling others how wonderful He is). Have you ever tried a product that brought such great results you recommended that your friends try it? When we testify about the goodness of God, by singing, shouting, or declaring His works, we are praising Him by recommendation. Not only does this help build our confidence in God, but it builds theirs also.

God loves diversity. That's why He made us all different. He has given us many different ways to praise Him. But one common thread applies to every form of praise: it cannot be hidden. It has to be heard or seen, or it's not praise. Praise is making a big to-do about God:

> Praise the Lord!
> Praise God in His sanctuary;
> Praise Him in His mighty firmament!
> Praise Him for His mighty acts;
> Praise Him according to His excellent
>   greatness!
> Praise Him with the sound of the
>   trumpet;
> Praise Him with the lute and harp!
> Praise Him with the timbrel and dance;
> Praise Him with stringed instruments
>   and flutes!
> Praise Him with loud cymbals;
> Praise Him with clashing cymbals!
> Let everything that has breath praise
>   the Lord. (Psalm 150:1–6)

If we are being honest, there are times when we don't feel like praising God. Singing, shouting, and dancing can be the furthest thing from our minds when life has us feeling beat down. However, praise is most important when our circumstances have

86

us feeling like complaining rather than proclaiming the goodness of God. When we praise Him in these times, we offer up "the sacrifice of praise" the Bible speaks about in Hebrews 13:15: "Therefore by Him let us continually offer the sacrifice of praise to God, that is, the fruit of our lips, giving thanks to His name." And yet, when we compare our earthly praise to the sacrifice He made for us on the cross, it doesn't seem like much of a sacrifice at all.

Daily Reflection

Read 2 Chronicles 20:1-23

- What was the result of praise?

Read Acts 16:22-26

- What caused the prison doors to become open?

Read Psalms 95:1, 6; 100:4; 149:3

- What are other ways to offer praise, according to these verses?

Application

God deserves our praise at all times, in every situation, and everywhere we go! Psalm 113:3 says, "From the rising of the sun to its going down, the LORD's name is to be praised." God doesn't tell us to praise Him because He needs to know how great He is; praise is for our own benefit. Praise is a powerful weapon that defeats the enemy—loosing chains and building our confidence in God.

Have you ever taken something of great value in to be appraised? It is examined carefully to determine the value. When we examine God carefully, taking in all that He is and all He has done, we will discover that He is invaluable—priceless. There is nothing worth more, nor could anything ever replace His value. He alone is worthy of all the praise!

WEEK 3

Hair

DAY 11

Hot Oil Treatment

Bessie Hicks

Behold, how good and how pleasant it is for brethren to dwell together in unity! It is like the precious oil upon the head, running down the beard, the beard of Aaron, running down on the edge of his garments.

PSALM 133:1–2

"My hair has been really dry lately from the blow-dryer and flat iron, and these split ends are driving me crazy," I said. "Is there anything you can do to help it?" I actually thought my hairdresser was going to tell me my hair needed to be cut off, so I was surprised at her answer: "Yes, there is! A good hot oil treatment can replenish, restore, and bring life back to your hair. It works by fusing the split ends back together before breakage takes place. It's as if it mends your hair back together."

Sometimes we need hot oil treatments in the Spirit. There are times when life can leave us dry, divided, or even broken. We, as the body of Christ, can end up being split like the ends of our hair. There is no place for division in the body of Christ. We are created to work and fit together. We need each other. The enemy works overtime, with every tool he has, to cause us to be offended and bring separation to the body. On the other hand, God has made every provision to bring us together in unity.

Our hair might seem like it would be an insignificant part, but it's important to God. He has every hair on our head numbered. There is no such thing as an insignificant part of His body. He wants every part to be fused together in love. When God pours the oil of the Holy Spirit over our lives, He brings refreshment and unity to every part of the body.

BEAUTY INSIDER TIP 1

It's the anointing that makes the difference

King David wrote Psalm 133 to show us a picture of how the oil (the anointing) is supposed to flow. In Old Testament times, when they anointed a prophet or a king, they would pour oil over his head. In ancient Israel, God not only anointed people; He also anointed things. The utensils in the tabernacle were anointed with oil, sanctified for the Lord's use. Once they were anointed, they were set apart never to be used again for ordinary purposes.

They were no longer ordinary. Instead, they were extraordinary as servants for the Lord. And once God anointed people, they were set apart for His use and purpose.

David understood this personally because when Samuel came to his father Jesse's house to anoint a king, he brought a horn of oil. While going through all of David's older, and seemingly more qualified, brothers, Samuel thought, *Surely this is God's choice for king.* However, none of them were God's choice. According to 1 Samuel 16:7, "The Lord does not see as man sees; for man looks at the outward appearance, but the Lord looks at the heart." David was described as a man after God's own heart (Acts 13:22). His pure heart was the reason the Spirit of the Lord eventually instructed Samuel to anoint David as the next king of Israel.

God has not changed. He is still looking to pour His anointing on the very one perhaps no one else would choose. He wants to do the same for us by pouring the oil of anointing over our lives. He no longer wants us to be used for the world but for His kingdom. He will not only anoint us personally; He will also anoint every ordinary thing in our lives. Whether it be a guitar, a sketchbook, or even our computer, God wants to anoint us, and everything pertaining to us, to use for His glory. The anointing—the oil being poured out from heaven—will take your ordinary and make it extraordinary!

BEAUTY INSIDER TIP 2

Unity is beautiful and valuable in God's sight

Let's look at Psalm 133:1 again, only this time in The Message version: "How wonderful, how beautiful, when brothers and sisters get along! It's like costly anointing oil flowing down." Think about our God, who created the heavens and earth; the maker of the majestic mountains and miles of ocean. If anyone could be considered a beauty expert, I think it's safe to say that He is. God knows beauty better than anyone—and nothing is more beautiful to God than watching His children get along. He delights in our unity, so much so that He likens it to costly anointing oil flowing down.

My friend Betty described the importance of unity between brothers when talking about her two oldest sons, who are as different as day and night. One has straight red hair; the other has curly blond hair. One son is older, the other one younger; and one is shy, while the other is outgoing. One is thin, and one is thick. One is serious; the other is silly. She could have gone on and on about their differences, yet each is her son. Betty loves them both equally, and her goal is to bind them together in love so that as they grow, they can help one another and witness to the world for the cause of Christ. "There is nothing that upsets me more than to see them fight with one another, or point out each other's differences, as a stance against one another," she said. "If this is how I feel, and I'm just a mother, imagine how God feels."

The way we treat each other is very important to God. We are not only His children but also His disciples. Jesus said in John 13:35, "By this all will know that you are My disciples, if you have love one for another." His love flowing through us sets us apart from the rest of the world. It's love that makes a difference. As born-again believers in Christ, we should not have to tell people we are Christians. The love and unity we have for each other should speak loud and clear, evident for all to see.

BEAUTY INSIDER TIP 3

Walking in unity brings great blessing

There are numerous references in the Bible that relate to the responsibilities we have toward one another. Some of the things He has instructed us to do are to love one another, encourage one another, and bear one another's burdens. The way we treat each other is a key factor to walking in unity. Through studying His Word, we get a clear understanding of how God would have us behave toward each other.

Galatians 5:13 says that we should serve one another. Let's not forget that the attitude and the heart behind our serving is also important. Can you imagine showing up to serve fellow believers in need and not treating them with kindness? Unfortunately, it happens all the time. Paul teaches in Romans 12:10, "Be kindly affectionate to one another with brotherly love, in honor giving preference to one another." These simple truths create unity among us and make way for the Spirit of the Lord to work for us and through us.

The Bible offers many benefits for walking in unity, one of them being a stronger prayer life. Prayer is powerful, but when we add agreement to that prayer, it becomes even more powerful. In Matthew 18:19 Jesus said, "If two of you agree on earth concerning anything that they ask, it will be done for them by My Father in heaven." Another promise is His presence. "For where two or three are gathered in My name, I am there with them" (v. 20).

Yes, it's true, God has promised to never leave us or forsake us, but there is a special corporate anointing that comes from being together with God's people in His name. We read in Ecclesiastes, "Two are better than one, because they have a good reward for their labor. For if they fall, one will lift up his companion. But woe to him who is alone when he falls, for he has no one to help him up. ... Though one may be overpowered by another, two can withstand him. And a threefold cord is not quickly broken" (4:9–10, 12). Unity with one another also has a good reward. We need each other.

Daily Reflection

Read John 13:34

- What is the new commandment the Lord gives?

Read Ephesians 4:30

- Why do you think it is important to forgive each other?

Read James 5:16

- What is a benefit of praying for one another?

Application

Like a blow-dryer that causes our ends to split, the enemy will always try to cause a split between the body of believers. But if we stick together by applying the oil of unity, we can stand against the attacks of the enemy. When we find ourselves stumbling, we, as believers, should be there to lift each other up and encourage one another. As a result, we will begin to see a body that is replenished, restored, and brought back to life.

DAY 12

Highlights & Lowlights

Betty Lovell

"Let your light so shine before men, that they may see your good works and glorify your Father in heaven."

MATTHEW 5:16

"We're going to bring you up nice and light," my hairdresser says to me every time I see her. Because of regrowth, I have to go back to the salon regularly to keep my hair as blonde as I like. I, like most women, like to look through magazines for models of different colors and styles. I have also brought in screenshots to show the look I'm trying to achieve. It makes me think, *What if we used Jesus as the model for our life?*

His Word should be the screenshot we carry around because His color is light and bright. He has the look we should be striving for. Jesus said, in Matthew 5:14, "A city that is set on a hill cannot be hidden." Why? Because it's bright. And He wants us to be that city shining bright for Him. He also says in verse 15, we don't "light a lamp and put it under a basket." Why? The candle brings light to all who are in the room. And, once again, He wants us to bring His light to all who are in the world. Today, we're going to use Jesus as our model to go light and bright.

BEAUTY INSIDER TIP 1

Set it and let it

You have a part to play—setting and letting. Most of us have our mind set before we let the stylist start cutting or coloring our hair. In the same way, in our relationship with Christ we must have our mind set that He is what we want for our life. We need to let Him become our example.

Philippians 2:5 says, "Let this mind be in you which was also in Christ Jesus." You decide. Who will you let rule your day? Will you let your own thoughts and emotions dictate all that you do? Or, will you set your mind on Christ and allow His thoughts and ways to flow through you? "If then you were raised with Christ, seek those things which are above, where Christ is, sitting at the right hand of God. Set your mind on things above, not on things on the earth" (Colossians 3:1–2). The instructions in these two verses are beyond valuable. It is time we get a different perspective. Sometimes, it is difficult to see past our own circumstances; but the apostle Paul encourages readers to expand their view.

There's no better view of New York City than from the top of the Empire State Building. From the ground, you see dirt, garbage, chaos, and hustle and bustle; but the next time you're in the Big Apple, I encourage you to take a step inside the strong tower. But don't stop there. Go straight to the top and look down at the city. With a different perspective, everything appears to be in perfect order.

God is the strong tower, and the righteous run to Him (Proverbs 18:10). Make up in your mind to go higher and set your mind on things above. Sometimes it can be hard to believe that God is working in your life when all you see is chaos and disarray. But when you set your mind on things above, renewing your mind in the Word, you'll get a different perspective. Run to Him and get a godly point of view with your eyes set on Christ.

There is a story in Luke 19 that tells of a tax collector named Zacchaeus. He was a short man who knew he had to get his eyes on Jesus. Because of his small stature, he could not see Jesus through the crowd, so what did he do? He ran ahead and climbed up into a sycamore tree because he purposed in his heart to set his eyes on Jesus. He just needed to get a little higher to catch a glimpse of the Savior walking by. He caught the attention of Jesus, who called out to him, "Zacchaeus, make haste and come down" (v. 5). Jesus not only called him by name but added, "For today I must stay at your house." The Savior came to dwell in the house of Zacchaeus—and according to verse 9, his entire household was saved that day.

What would you do if Jesus came to stay at your house? I thought about what I like to do when I have company. I try to make it a point to wake up early to spend time with my guests. Having my morning tea (or coffee) with them is especially nice if we can make it up before the children do. It is a time for conversations you can't have when there are more people around. It is a time for listening, venting, testifying, giving advice, laughing, and discussing our plans for the day—and even our plans for the future. Why would I treat my Lord and Savior, who dwells in my heart (Ephesians 3:17), any different?

BEAUTY INSIDER TIP 2

Let's go higher and dwell there!

One of the most well-known portions of Scripture is Psalm 91. It's packed full of the promises of God, including deliverance, protection, and much more. Allow me to draw your attention to verse 9: "You have made the Lord, who is my refuge, even the Most High, your dwelling place." A dwelling place is a home or a habitation. It's the place where you abide, not just somewhere you visit. Some Christians are satisfied with a once-a-week visit on Sunday morning, but we can make the Most High our dwelling place.

When you read through the rest of Psalm 91, you'll see what can be expected of those who make God their dwelling place. In the following verses, He promises that no evil shall overtake us or plague get close to our dwelling (v. 10). He gives His angels charge over us to keep us in all our ways (v. 11). Because we have set our love upon Him, He will set us on high (v. 14). He says that when we call upon Him, He will answer us and be with us in times of trouble (v. 15). Finally, He promises to satisfy us with long life and show us His salvation (v. 16).

At the time of salvation, Christ comes to dwell in our hearts through faith. By acknowledging His presence, we make him our dwelling place. Ephesians 2:6 says God has "raised us up together, and made us sit together in the heavenly places in Christ Jesus." Heavenly places are high above the earthly circumstances of everyday life. In Him, we can rise above everything that tries to pull us down.

BEAUTY INSIDER TIP 3

Bring it low to bring it high

Have you ever noticed that highlights stand out more on darker hair? Many women will get lowlights put in their hair to make the highlights stand out. The highlights are brighter against the darker color. It is much the same way with the voice of God. When the sun has not quite started to rise, and the light is low, His voice seems to be much clearer and tends to stand out. In the darkness of the morning, there's a stillness and a calm, not only in your home, but in the world around you. The Bible says, in Isaiah 50:4, "He awakens Me morning by morning."

The psalmist said it like this: "O God, You are my God; early will I seek You; my soul thirsts for You; my flesh longs for You in a dry and thirsty land where there is no water" (Psalm 63:1). By getting up early to seek the face of God, we are automatically looking up. Have you ever woken up just 15 minutes later than you should have? It seems to throw your whole day off, making it feel hurried and rushed. The way your morning starts sets the rest of your day in motion.

Most of us are familiar with the Proverbs 31 woman. The Bible says, "She also rises while it is yet night, and provides food for her household, and a portion for her maidservants." She was not the only one that rose early to seek the Lord. You will actually find several examples of people throughout the Word who got up early to seek God, even our perfect model, Jesus. "In the early morning, while it was still dark, Jesus got up, left the house, and went away to a secluded place, and was praying there" (Mark 1:35 NASB).

In the morning, we need wisdom, knowledge, and understanding because when the sun comes up, the day starts. The husband and children wake up, the phone starts ringing, and bills need to be paid; and that's not to mention the commute to work or the list of household chores. There's just not enough time in the day to do all that is needed. Take a page from Jesus' book— be an early riser. I don't know of anyone who was busier, or had more to do, than Jesus—but He made it a point to seek God early in the morning.

Daily Reflection

Read Luke 19:1-10

- What are some things you can do to get closer to the Lord?

Read Psalm 91:9-19

- Pick two promises from this psalm and meditate on them today.

Read Psalm 5:3

- What is David's promise to the Lord in this psalm?

Application

I cannot stress to you enough the importance of seeking the face of God. We learned today that we are to set our affections on things above. Set your mind in the morning, and keep it set for the day. Just like you wouldn't dream of sitting in the chair at the salon without already having your mind set on what you want, don't start your day without having your mind set on Christ. Rising early to pray changes your perspective, sets your affections on things above, and will "let this mind be in you which is also in Christ Jesus" (Philippians 2:5).

DAY 13

Trim It Up

Mary Burden

"I am the true Vine, and My Father is the vinedresser. Every branch in Me that does not bear fruit, He takes away; and every branch that continues to bear fruit, He [repeatedly] prunes, so that it will bear more fruit [even richer and finer fruit]."

JOHN 15:1-2 (AMP)

After I get a hair treatment, my hairdresser will usually ask, "Are you ready for a trim?" My typical response is, "No, not today. I don't have time for a trim. Just give me a quick blow-dry and I'll be fine. I'm in a hurry, and I've been trying to let it grow out." With years of experience, my stylist never fails to remind me, "It will not grow healthy if we don't take off these dead ends." Even though I know the stylist knows more about hair than I do, it just doesn't seem logical that I would have to cut my dead ends off to make my hair grow.

Now let's consider the hairdresser in comparison to the Vinedresser. God is our Vinedresser, and He knows that we have dead things in our life that must be trimmed. If these dead things are not pruned back, they will cause the whole tree to be polluted, resulting in the death of the tree. You have been given the Master stylist, the Creator of the earth, the one who formed you in your mother's womb. What concerns you concerns Him. He says, "The very hairs on your head are all numbered" (Matthew 10:30). He desires to see you grow and produce much fruit.

Often, when it is time for trimming our dead ends off, we say, "Not now, Lord. I'm in a hurry. I'm going to try and let it grow on its own." Yet every season we come back, and we have not grown an inch. We fall into the same shortcomings and pitfalls, and then wonder, *Why am I not growing in the Lord? Why am I not producing the fruits of the Spirit?* At times like these, we need to make a choice. Do we allow the Vinedresser to prune us, or trim us, or do we continue to walk around as a dead end? Ultimately, the choice is ours. We can follow expert advice (the Word of God) or choose our own will.

BEAUTY INSIDER TIP 1

Use preventive measures

Our hairdressers advise us to have a little trim to prevent us from losing the whole strand of hair and to allow healthy and strong hair to grow. Our Vinedresser also desires to trim us. The trimming back is not just to take away from us, but He desires to trim off the things that could cause spiritual harm to make room for growth in Him. He wants to catch the small foxes before they spoil the vine (Song of Solomon 2:15). He uses the Word of God to instruct us and His Spirit to guide us. He uses them to prevent us from being lured away, by the enemy, to a dead-end place. I once heard a story, from a friend, that reminded me of this.

One day, she and a friend were swimming in a calm little bay on the beaches of Hawaii. She had been warned by the lifeguard to stay away from the buoys. There was a strong current out that day, and three people had already been rescued from that area. As she and her friend swam out to look at fish, not paying attention, they began to feel the strong pull of the current. She realized they had started to drift into the very area they had been warned about. Since she was a strong swimmer, she swam her way out of the current into calmer water, which was not as easy as she thought it would be. She realized how easily she could have been swept into the ocean and drowned. She shared a testimony about how she had gotten busy in her own life. While taking care of day-to-day things, she found herself drifting from the Lord. She realized the dangers of not keeping a watch over her own heart.

I have a similar testimony in my own life. I was a born-again believer, being used in service to the Lord, and I had (or so I thought) a good solid relationship with God. When I had my first child, I got into a busy season of life. For most women, having a new baby brings a new, hectic schedule. I was not careful, and I allowed the blessings the Lord had given me to rob me of the time I used to spend with Him. I wasn't doing anything bad, but my life had become out of balance. Instead of spending my time studying my Bible and worshiping the Lord every day, I was looking for the newest baby products out, getting together with other new moms, and obsessing over planning my son's future.

Don't misunderstand what I'm saying. There's nothing wrong with any of these things, but everything we do must be done in balance. This is why God tells us, in His Word, to "seek first the kingdom of God and His righteousness, and all these things shall be added to you" (Matthew 6:33). He gives us these instructions to prevent us from falling into a trap of the enemy. He knows we have need of all these things, but He wants us to put Him first, and all these things will follow.

"Be sober [well balanced and self-disciplined], be alert and cautious at all times. That enemy of yours, the devil, prowls around like a roaring lion [fiercely hungry], seeking someone to devour" (1 Peter 5:8 AMP). This is a warning from God. He is trying to show us, through His Word, how to prevent an attack from the enemy. He tells us to be well balanced and alert because our enemy is like a roaring lion. Lions are flesh eaters. When we walk after the flesh, we leave ourselves wide open to be devoured by the enemy. According to Galatians 5:16, however, if we walk in the Spirit, we will "not fulfill the lust of the flesh."

Jesus speaks a parable to the disciples in Mark chapter 4 where He relates the human heart to the sowing of seeds. In verses 18 and 19, this is what He has to say about the ones that were sown among thorns: "They are the ones who hear the word, and the cares of this world, the deceitfulness of riches, and the desires for other things entering in choke the word, and it becomes unfruitful." I realized I had been allowing the cares of this life to choke my time spent with the Lord and my time in His Word. I became unfruitful to the kingdom of God. I was trying to hold on to the things of the Lord with one hand and the things of the world with the other. I was much like my friend in that I had drifted into the strong current. I found myself in a place I couldn't get myself out of. As a result, I ended up in condemnation, not allowing myself to be used for the kingdom of God.

BEAUTY INSIDER TIP 2

Stop loving the dead ends

In Judges 13–16, we find the well-known story of Samson. He was a man called, before he was born, to deliver the Israelite people from the Philistines. His mother had taken the Nazirite vow, and he was not allowed to shave his hair. Although Samson was called by God, he struggled with obedience and making the right choices in his life. Staying true to his lifestyle of disobedience, he took a wife from the Philistines, even though his mother and father had instructed him to take a wife from his own people. He also disobeyed the vow of the Nazirite by touching unclean animals.

Despite his wrong choices, God's Spirit still came upon him and gave him the strength to fight off thirty Philistine men. Again and again, God's Spirit would come upon Samson and he would do great things. Eventually Samson's lust of the flesh leads him into a dead-end place. He fell in love with a woman named Delilah, and she lured him right into a trap that would cost him everything. After she asked him three times, Samson finally gave in and told Delilah where his great strength lay.

As he fell asleep, she called for the Philistines to shave his head. Once all his locks of hair were gone, "she began to torment him, and his strength left him. And she said, 'The Philistines are upon you, Samson!' So, he awoke from his sleep, and said, 'I will go out as before, at other times, and shake myself free!' But he did not know that the LORD had departed from him" (16:20). Samson's love for the things of this world had lured him so far from the call of God on his life that he didn't even realize the Spirit of God had departed from him.

The enemy still uses the same tricks to lead God's people down dead-end paths. "There is a way which seems right to a man, but its end is the way of death" (Proverbs 14:12).

BEAUTY INSIDER TIP 3

Cry out to God, and it will grow again

When Samson was captured by the Philistines, he did what we should do when we find ourselves in a dead-end place: he cried out to the Lord. Psalm 18:6 says, "In my distress I called upon the LORD, and cried unto my God: he heard my voice out of his temple, and my cry came before him, even into his ears" (KJV). Although Samson made many mistakes, when he cried out to the Lord, He heard his cry and empowered him once again. From his mother's womb, God had a purpose for Samson's life. Judges 13:5 says, "He shall begin to deliver Israel out of the hand of the Philistines."

Even though Samson had lost his strength, and had his eyes taken out, God was not done with him yet. The Bible says that Samson's hair began to grow again, and he called out to the Lord, "O Lord God, remember me, I pray thee, and strengthen me, I pray thee, only this once, O God, that I may be at once avenged of the Philistines for my two eyes" (Judges 16:28 KJV). That day, three thousand Philistine leaders gathered together to make sport out of Samson. All they could see was a weak blind man, and they counted him out.

It appeared that the God of Samson had turned His back on him, but God was faithful. With a boy's help, Samson placed his hands on the two pillars, then shook the very foundation of that place. The three thousand leaders who had gathered together to make sport of Samson all died that day. "So the dead which he slew at his death were more than they which he slew in his life" (v. 30 KJV). Samson did more for Israel that day than throughout the entire course of his life.

Daily Reflection

Read John 15:1-2

- In what areas of your life can you use a trim?

Read Judges 13-16

- Have you invested too much time into something that is causing your life to become out of balance?

Read Psalm 18:6

- When is the last time you cried out to the Lord?

Application

I thank God for the truth of His Word and His loving mercy. When I found myself drifting into a dead-end place, the Word of God came out of the depths of my heart. Quoting Romans 8:38-39, I would say, "Nothing can separate me from your love, Lord. Nothing can separate me from your love!" I cried out unto the Lord, and He heard me. I too began to grow again. I started renewing my mind in the Word daily, and I spent time in church, fellowshiping with other believers. One finger at a time, I began to let go of the cares of this world. I put both hands to the plow and never looked back. Thank God, I haven't found myself in that dead-end place again.

My prayer for you is that you would allow the Vinedresser to trim off the dead ends in your life. I challenge you today to allow Him to prune you. And I promise you'll be pleased with the growth.

DAY 14

Blow-Dry

Mary Burden

*"Behold, I send the Promise of My Father upon you;
but tarry in the city of Jerusalem until you are
endued with power from on high."*

LUKE 24:49

I am often in a hurry and try to skip out on the blow-dry. My hair-dresser gets very confused by this. I can tell what she's thinking: *Sure, you can leave without it, but why would you want to? It's included with all your other treatments.* The look on her face says it all: *Is this really the look you're going for?* Leaving without my hair blow-dried and styled just seems foolish to her. Most hair (especially mine), when left to air-dry, becomes curly and unruly, with no shape or style. It gets really wild and defiant and needs to be tamed to look presentable. Someone else's hair might dry limp and flat to the head, with no volume at all.

BEAUTY INSIDER TIP 1

Connect to the power

Our world was very different before the 1800s, when electricity had not yet been discovered. The world fully functioned and was productive without it, but the discovery of electricity revolutionized the world. Electric power has changed the way most people do everything. We no longer light candles at night to see, heat our water on a wood-burning stove for a bath, or beat our clothes against a rock to wash them. Praise God for that! But did you know there are still people living on this earth who have access to power but choose to live without it?

This is how the world was before the Holy Spirit was fully given. The Holy Spirit, who is our power source, has been here since the beginning (Genesis 1:2). However, it was not until Jesus ascended that the Holy Spirit came to abide inside the heart of all those who would receive Him. "But you shall receive power when the Holy Spirit has come upon you; and you shall be witnesses to Me in Jerusalem, and in all Judea and Samaria, and to the end of the earth," (Acts 1:8). Now this gift of the Holy Spirit has been freely given to anyone who will receive Him. As we learned in "Moisturizer," when we are baptized in His Spirit, we are filled with His power.

Why would we ever choose to live without Him? We can have all the right tools at hand to mold and shape our hair, but if we don't plug into the power source, we will never know what it is like to be molded and shaped by them. God is the source from which all power comes. The Holy Spirit is the chord that releases the power of God from heaven to us. He then releases that power, through us, to a lost and dying world. He is the root of the fruit of the Spirit; the power source from which love, joy, peace, and *all* spiritual gifts flow.

BEAUTY INSIDER TIP 2

Become windblown and fire shaped

The Bible says the disciples followed Jesus' instruction and waited in Jerusalem until they received power from on high. The day finally arrived, and as they gathered together in unity and prayer, there came a sound like a mighty rushing wind and the fire of the Holy Ghost fell on *all* who were there:

> When the Day of Pentecost had fully come, they were all with one accord in one place. And suddenly there came a sound from heaven, as of a rushing mighty wind, and it filled the whole house where they were sitting. Then there appeared to them divided tongues, as of fire, and one sat upon each of them. And they were all filled with the Holy Spirit and began to speak with other tongues, as the Spirit gave them utterance. (Acts 2:1–4)

The most powerful tool we have been given is our mouth. That's why it's should not be a surprise that the first evidence of receiving the Holy Spirit is a spoken utterance. God has given us the same tool He used. When the mouth of God spoke, light came (Genesis 1:3). When Jesus spoke, the winds obeyed (Mark 4:39); when He cursed the fig tree, it shriveled up and died (11:14). We are made in the image of God. With our tongue, He has given us the power to create life or death. He has also given us the power to release blessings or curses over our lives.

Have you ever had hair that is untamable—the type that when it's air-dried seems to have a mind of its own? Maybe you have a cowlick that has naturally grown in one direction, and no matter what you do, it just goes right back in the same place. That stubborn hair will not even stay down with a hair product. It takes the heat of the blow-dryer or flat iron to tame it and point it in the right direction.

Our tongue is the same way. It naturally speaks evil, lies, gossips, and boasts. It is 100 percent flesh, and no one can tame it. However, as we yield to the fire of the Holy Spirit and allow Him to finish the work He has started (Philippians 1:6), this untamable part of our body can be molded and shaped, becoming one of the most powerful and effective tools for the kingdom of God. The book of James teaches that our mouth is a very small piece of our body. Yet, like the rudder of a boat, which steers the whole ship, our tongue boasts great things and steers our whole body.

That's why the fire that fell upon those sitting in the upper room on the day of Pentecost was so important. Their tongues were the first part of them to be affected. By surrendering their mouths to the power of the Holy Spirit, they were presenting themselves unto God as a living sacrifice.

BEAUTY INSIDER TIP 3

Blow-drying brings volume

Another reason for blow-drying is to add volume to your hair. When the wind and fire of the Holy Spirit blew through the upper room, it brought volume to the voices who received it. "But Peter, standing up with the eleven, raised his voice and said to them, 'Men of Judaea and all who dwell in Jerusalem, let this be known unto you, and heed my words'" (Acts 2:14). Peter, a disciple of Jesus, began speaking before thousands with a loud voice, full of boldness. This may seem like a normal thing for a disciple, but not for Peter.

A few months prior to this, Jesus had been brought before the high priest Caiaphas, and Peter wasn't even bold enough to stand up for Him. He fled, along with the other disciples. As a matter of fact, Peter wasn't even bold enough to stand up to a servant girl who recognized him as one of the disciples. He was asked three times, by three different people, if he was one of the followers of Jesus. He lied and denied Jesus each time, cursing and swearing to prove he was not a disciple (Matthew 26:69–75).

Once Peter was filled with the Spirit, however, we never see this fearful, cowardly side of him again. That tongue of his, the same one he used to deny Jesus three times, was tamed by the Holy Spirit. Peter is now in the same town and speaking to the same people. There is something different this time though—he is filled with Holy Ghost power! For the first time ever recorded, Peter raised the volume of his voice and boldly proclaimed the Word of God. He quoted from Joel 2:28, a prophetic passage explaining the outpouring of the Spirit that they were experiencing.

Instead of Peter denying he knew Jesus, he was teaching those around him and proclaiming the gospel of Christ. Because of Peter's raised voice, three thousand souls were added to the church that day. Hallelujah! The Bible tells us in Acts 4 that when the people saw the courage of Peter and John and realized they were unschooled, ordinary men, they were astonished and took note that these men had been with Jesus.

When you leave a hair salon, with your fresh highlights and your blown-out hair, it becomes apparent that you have been with a stylist. Those who have seen you in the past week or so with your ponytail and your grown-out roots recognize a difference. You start to hear things like, "You look lovely and fresh. Did you get your hair done? Who did your highlights? What salon do you go to?" Just by allowing the stylist to complete the work she started, you become a witness to her work, which can result in new clients for her.

The believers who were filled at Pentecost were ordinary, ignorant, and unlearned, but they allowed the Holy Spirit to do a complete work in them and He became their teacher. He moved through them, making them the most effective witnesses possible. Under the unction of the Holy Spirit, they were able to perform many miracles, heal the sick, and speak with boldness. They moved from the cowardly to the courageous, resulting in multiple souls being added to the kingdom of God.

Peter and John were not the only ones who moved in the power of the Spirit. Many others, like Stephen and Philip, were empowered to be witnesses of the saving power of Jesus. God does not tell us that we have power to be his lawyer. He actually doesn't need us to argue on his behalf. However, He does tell us we are empowered to be His witnesses. Remember Jesus' words in Acts 1:8 ("You shall receive power ... and you shall be witnesses to Me")? There is nothing more powerful in a court of law than an eyewitness—one who is willing to testify to the truth of what they have seen and experienced with their own eyes. An eyewitness will win over hearsay in any court.

The Holy Spirit has come to give you the boldness you need to be His witnesses here on earth. He wants to enable you and equip you to be a witness of the saving grace of His love. James 1:17 says, "Every good gift and every perfect gift is from above, and comes down from the Father of lights." Will you accept this gift? Please don't neglect this gift of the Holy Spirit. After all, what good is a gift if it's never received?

Daily Reflection

Read Acts 1:8

- What does the Holy Spirit give you the power to do?

Read James 3:4–12

- What does James liken the tongue to?

Read Luke 11:13

- What gift does the Lord want to give to you?

Application

When I walk out of the salon with my hair wet, refusing the complete package, I end up with shapeless, unruly hair, which is foolish. Even more foolish is not allowing the Lord to complete the work He has started in you. The power source is there; all you must do is tap into it. Imagine a life where you are tongue tamed, windblown, and fire shaped. With the Holy Spirit working through you to be a power-*full* witness for the kingdom of God, that's exactly who you will be.

The Lord is offering you a free gift of the Holy Spirit today. If you have never been filled with the Holy Spirit (with the evidence of speaking in tongues), or you need a refreshing, we invite you to receive your gift today. Please refer to the back of the book to accept this invitation.

DAY 15

Hairspray

Bessie Hicks

The LORD is a stronghold for the oppressed,
a stronghold in times of trouble.

PSALM 9:9 (ESV)

"I'm just about done. All I have to do is add the finishing touch. Will you pass me the hairspray? The one that says 'Stronghold.' I don't want this hair going anywhere." My stylist makes me laugh, always insisting on making sure every hair stays exactly where she placed it. All her hard work highlighting, trimming, and blowing it into shape will be a waste if she doesn't set it in place. With hairspray, it will last for the rest of the day, sometimes two.

Before we spray our hair, we still have the option of changing our look. We may usually have it blown out straight, but it's a woman's prerogative to change her mind. So we decided to add a few curls. When we're satisfied with the changes, having made up our mind on the look we're after, we want to set it. Now it's up to the hairspray to keep the style in place. We need something that's going to hold up under any weather conditions or whatever we may face throughout the day.

BEAUTY INSIDER TIP 1

The Lord is our stronghold

It's a pretty tall order to expect a spray to keep your hair in place through anything. But when it comes to the things of the Spirit, God is able to uphold us with His mighty hand. "I will strengthen you," He says in Isaiah 41:10. "Yes, I will help you, I will uphold you with My righteous right hand." No matter what life throws at us, if we will commit our lives to Him, He will keep that which has been committed to Him.

The Bible is full of verses that refer to God as your stronghold or fortress. David wrote in Psalm 144:2, "My lovingkindness and my fortress, my high tower and my deliverer, my shield ... in whom I take refuge." He is your source of strength, and you can always rely on Him. No matter how weak you may feel, you can rest assured, knowing His grace is "sufficient for you" and His strength is "made perfect" in your weakness (2 Corinthians 12:9).

One of the tactics of the enemy is to wear out, or wear down, the saints (Daniel 7:25). He will try to weaken you. When you're tired or weak, he will come tempt you. But Paul instructs us in Ephesians 6:10, "Be strong in the Lord and in the power of His might."

We're not in this alone; Jesus also faced temptation from the enemy. In Matthew 4, He had been fasting for 40 days and was hungry. Satan tried to tempt Jesus into turning the stones to bread to satisfy His hunger. He was trying to provoke the Lord into caving to His weakness. Jesus made sure the enemy knew exactly where His strength was coming from but starting with, "It is written ..." (v. 4). The Word will give you strength to defeat satan every time.

BEAUTY INSIDER TIP 2

The enemy works hard to set up strongholds

There is another stronghold in the Bible, and this one comes from the enemy. Everything God does, the enemy tries to counterfeit. God is the Creator. Satan is the imitator. Using his own strongholds, he will try to set you up and hold you captive. The first place satan will try to tempt you is in your mind. He knows if he can get you to think about something long enough, he can get you to do it. He wants to gain control of your actions. He does this by setting up strongholds in your mind. Behind every stronghold from satan is a lie; he's the father of all lies (John 8:44).

A stronghold is built upon something that you believe. If it is a stronghold from God, it comes from believing the Word of God. If it comes from the enemy, it stems from believing a lie that is contrary to the Word of God. This is why it's important to have your mind renewed through the Word. The more truth you know, the fewer lies you'll believe. Only the truth can defeat a lie. Satan often starts to set up these strongholds in your mind at a young age. For this reason, it is imperative that you teach your children the truth of God's Word.

I once heard of how a ten-thousand-pound elephant can be tied down with nothing more than a rope and a stake. When the baby elephant is born (to keep him from escaping), a rope is placed around him and is staked to the ground. When he is still little, the baby elephant will try to break free from the rope that has him bound. But he can't. The rope is too strong for him. After many failed attempts to break free, he simply won't try anymore; he's convinced the rope will always be stronger.

Elephants are known for having a good memory. As a matter of fact, they can remember watering holes from years ago and lead their families there for survival. We also have long-term memories. We have the ability to recall things from years back, but not everything we remember is for our benefit. Some things need to be cast into the sea of forgetfulness (Micah 7:19). You have to be careful not to allow these memories to be a foundation for a stronghold in your mind. Past hurts, failures, or even insulting words that were spoken over you can be something the enemy uses to try to keep you bound.

When the elephant grows up, he is way stronger than the rope that ties him down. But because it tried to break free before and failed, he ends up living in bondage. The elephant is actually only bound in his mind, by its way of thinking. That's how a stronghold from the enemy works. But here's the good news: God has given us mighty weapons to pull down strongholds!

BEAUTY INSIDER TIP 3

We can pull down
the enemy's strongholds

"For the weapons of our warfare are not carnal but mighty in God for the pulling down of strongholds, casting down [imaginations] and every high thing that exalts itself against the knowledge of God, bringing every thought into captivity to the obedience of Christ" (2 Corinthians 10:4–5).

God has given you powerful weapons to tear down the devil's strongholds. You are no match for the enemy on your own, but as Paul said, "You can do all things through Christ who strengthens [you]" (Philippians 4:19). These weapons are not carnal (fleshly) weapons; they are spiritual weapons. They have the ability to destroy every stronghold when you learn to use them properly. One weapon used to pull down these strongholds is the truth of the Word of God.

Let's be honest. We all have strongholds of some kind. We have areas in our mind where we believe the lies the enemy tells us. We might not recognize it as that; it may just seem like stinkin' thinkin'. But if it's been there a while, it might be a stronghold. There can be a number of different thoughts that fill your mind: fear, anger, insecurity, pride, anxiety, or unforgiveness. The list could go on and on.

As you are reading this, you may be thinking, *Yes, I have some of these thoughts, but doesn't everyone? How am I supposed to change my way of thinking? They're constantly in my mind, so how do I pull them down, and what does it mean to cast down imaginations?* According to *Strong's Concordance*, to pull down means "to demolish or lower." You will notice the instruction in the Bible to destroy strongholds means to pull down and cast down every high thing. The lies of satan must be lowered. The truth of God's Word must be lifted up, taking its proper place in your mind. The Bible refers to God as the Most High. It also says that His thoughts are higher than our thoughts (Isaiah 55:9). You can put on the mind of Christ, making His thoughts

124

become your thoughts. Philippians 2:5 says, "Let this mind be in you which was also in Christ Jesus."

Isaiah 14:12–14 gives us a glimpse into what caused Lucifer to fall from being an angel in heaven to the prince of darkness that we know as the devil. He said, "I will ascend into heaven, I will exalt my throne; ... I will ascend above the heights of the clouds. I will be like the Most High." His desire was to replace God, to be higher than Him, so he looks for any opportunity to exalt himself. When you listen to satan's lies, you allow them to be exalted above God's promises. But you can pull down these strongholds. You can cast down every thought that is contrary to the Word of God by replacing them with the promises found in the Word of God.

When the enemy is telling you that God doesn't love you, you can remind him that according to John 3:16 and Romans 8:35–37, God loves you so much He sent His Son to die for you. When he tries to convince you that your sins are not forgiven, you can tell him how He has removed your sin as far as the east is from the west (Psalm 103:12). When he's got you bound by fear and trying to make you believe you're losing your mind, speak out 2 Timothy 1:7, for God has given you a sound mind, not a spirit of fear.

While the list of lies can certainly go on and on, the truth will always defeat the lies—if you refuse to believe them. Know the truth, think on the truth, and replace the lies in your head with the truth of His Word. In Philippians 4:8 you will find specific instruction on what we are to be thinking about: things that are true, noble, just, pure, lovely, virtuous, praiseworthy, or of good report. Follow these instructions, and you will pull down the strongholds in your mind.

Daily Reflection

Read 2 Timothy 1:12

- Do you believe God will keep all that you commit to Him?

Read John 8:44-45

- Who is the liar and who tells the truth?

Read Philippians 4:6-8

- What are some of the things this passage is instructing you to think about?

Application

We opened today's study with the example of using stronghold hairspray to keep your hair in place. Regardless of how much time you put into styling your hair, if you fail to use hairspray, it will go right back to the way it was before you started.

Learning to set your mind and keep it set works the same way. You must consistently renew your mind with the Word of God (Romans 12:2) to keep strongholds from the enemy from forming. If you allow yourself to think on whatever pops in your head, you will see very little change in your life. You will allow the enemy to control your thoughts, inadvertently allowing him to control your life. Let the Lord be your stronghold. If you set your mind on Him, the Word promises He will keep you in perfect peace (Isaiah 26:3). And 2 Timothy 1:12 says He is able to keep that which has been committed to Him.

WEEK 4

The Spa

DAY 16

Manicure

Annie Smith

*"For this thing the L*ORD *your God will bless you in all your works and in all to which you put your hand."*

DEUTERONOMY 15:10

Isn't it funny how some people's hands can almost tell a story? Some look dry, brittle, and hard, while others can be soft, smooth, and polished. Take a look at your hands. What do you think they would say about you? For me, the story my hands tell would depend on whether I have recently had a manicure. If it has been a while, they would tell the story of a busy mom who is not will- ing to take the time for herself and sit for a manicure. When I have a fresh manicure, it's usually because I have a function to attend and I would like to look clean and polished. At these times, I'm willing to spend time in the manicure chair. Whatever way you see your hands, I can almost guarantee that you don't see them as God sees them.

To God, beautiful hands are willing hands. When your hands are dry and chipped, and you need a manicure, you must be willing to go to the salon and sit in the chair. You have to place your hands in the hands of the manicurist and trust her not to harm you while she's cutting, clipping, shaping, and removing your cuticles. Eventually your skin becomes softened—but there's a process to making them beautiful, and it starts with your will. The Spirit of God wants to give you a spiritual manicure, but it also depends upon you handing yourself over to Him. Are you willing to?

BEAUTY INSIDER TIP 1

Are you willing to learn?

God wants to teach us to use our hands for Him. "If you listen to advice and are willing to learn, one day you will be wise" (Proverbs 19:20 GNT). King David wasn't always a wise, mighty, valiant warrior. He started as a shepherd boy in the field, tending to his father's flock and running errands. But one of the things that made David so special was his willingness to learn. He said in Psalm 144:1, "Blessed be the name of the LORD my strength which teacheth my hands to war, and my fingers to fight" (KJV).

Even after David was anointed to be king, he did not cease to learn the Word of God. In Psalm 18:22, David spoke about a time when he was delivered from the hand of Saul, saying, "For all [God's] judgments were before me, and I did not put away His statutes from me." He was constantly learning the Word of

God. This little shepherd boy grew to be a great king and warrior for God. You too can become, like David, a force to be reckoned with—if you're willing to learn.

BEAUTY INSIDER TIP 2

Are you willing to work with your hands?

Most of us are familiar with the Proverbs 31 woman, the "virtuous wife" (v. 10). Not only do these verses describe the type of wife we should be to our husbands, but they give us a picture of the bride of Christ. Verse 13 says she "willingly works with her hands." The Lord's desire is for us to willingly work on His behalf. He is a gentleman though and would never force us to do anything we're not willing to do.

Genesis 24 tells a story about Abraham sending his servant to look for a bride for his son Isaac. Before the servant left, he asked Abraham, "Perhaps the woman will not be willing to follow me to this land. Must I take your son back to the land from which you came?" (v. 5). Abraham answered, "If the woman is not willing to follow you, then you will be released from this oath" (v. 8). The servant obeyed his master's instructions and came to a well of water. He would ask a young woman for a drink, and if she offered water for his camels also, he would know she was the one. Rebekah, who was there drawing water for her family, did just that. She didn't even ask if he wanted water for his camels. After giving water to Abraham's servant, she simply said, "I will draw water for your camels also" (v. 19) and began to draw and serve more water.

As the bride of Christ, we should be willing to serve the water of the Word to a stranger. I love how verse 16 describes

Rebekah as "beautiful to behold." I think what made her beauty so apparent was her willingness to serve. She was already a worker before the servant showed up on the scene, filling pots for her family. It says a lot about her character that she was not only willing to work for her family, but she went above and beyond for a complete stranger and his camels. The average camel can drink about thirty gallons of water in thirteen minutes, and she drew enough for ten camels! That is what made Rebekah beautiful, inside and out.

In the book of Luke, chapter 10, we find the parable of the good Samaritan, a man who was willing to serve in so many ways. He offered to clean, bandage, and dress wounds for a complete stranger. Like Rebekah, he went above and beyond for someone he had never met. He set the injured man on his own animal, then brought him to an inn to take care of him. He also promised to repay any debt the man would accumulate. In other words, the Good Samaritan was willing to work with his hands by getting involved. What a beautiful picture of Christ we find in this story!

I once heard a testimony about a young man who dropped out of college to follow God's will and become a preacher. As a result, his father became very bitter and rude toward him, refusing to talk to him. Yet the preacher continued to share the gospel with his father, who didn't want to hear it. The father was later diagnosed with cancer. In his last days, his preacher son came to take care of him, willingly serving his father in a hands-on way to spare his father the embarrassment of the nurses having do it for him. You can use your imagination as to the things he had to do. But the preacher said that as he served his father, it softened his heart and made way for him to ask his father to accept the Lord— one last time. That preacher had the privilege of leading his father to the Lord because of his willingness to work with his hands.

BEAUTY INSIDER TIP 3

Are you willing to give?

Look at your hands: God has blessed you with two for a reason. It's possible to give different things out of each, and at the same time. But most of us find it difficult to just give out of one. There's a man in the Old Testament named Nehemiah, who was willing to give when he saw his people in need—a perfect example of a man of great character who gave out of both hands at the same time. He and his team built a wall while prepared to fight off the enemy: "Those who built on the wall, and those who carried burdens, loaded themselves so that with one hand they worked on construction, and with the other held a weapon" (Nehemiah 4:17).

You might be thinking you have enough burdens in your personal life and can't imagine taking on someone else's. But read that verse again. Did you notice the ones who were working with one hand and their weapon in the other were carrying burdens also? If they could work and be ready to fight while loaded down with burdens, why can't we?

When most of us think of giving, our mind goes to money and gifts. Yes, I'm talking about giving those things, but the Lord wants to go deeper than monetary value. I'm also talking about giving your time to build up people who have been torn down. I'm talking about fighting in the Spirit for those who aren't strong enough to fight for themselves. I'm talking about showing love, mercy, and kindness to others. But most importantly, I'm talking about taking time to invest in someone's life.

Don't wait until your life is perfect to pour into someone in need. If we all did that, I'm afraid we would never be able to give.

Daily Reflection

Read Genesis 24:11-27

- What made Rebekah stand out to Abraham's servant?

Read Luke 10:23-35

- In how many different areas was the Good Samaritan willing to work with his hands?

Read Nehemiah 4:17

- What could you be doing more to give?

Application

Look at your hands again. What do you see? I'm hoping you see hands that are willing to learn, willing to work, willing to give, and willing to get dirty and fight! Hands the Lord has blessed you with for the purpose of blessing those around you. There's so much beauty the Lord has given us through our hands; we haven't even begun to scratch the surface. But first, you must make up your mind—are you willing?

Pedicure

Laura Wharton

*"How beautiful are the feet of those
who preach the gospel of peace."*

ROMANS 10:15

We all love to be pampered. I'm sure I'm not the only woman reading this who enjoys a good pedicure. Most of the time, I don't want to get out of the chair when it's over. Oh, the feeling of having all that old dead skin removed and the oil massaged in, making my feet soft and smooth. We can't forget about the coat of polish, which makes them look as beautiful as they feel. What a great feeling to walk out of the nail salon so refreshed and clean! Isn't it funny how even though the rest of your body wasn't touched, just having your feet scrubbed can make you feel clean and peaceful?

Did you know that the Lord really cares about your feet? He actually spoke about them several times throughout the Bible. He associated our feet with peace through the apostle Paul, who instructed the believers in Ephesus to fit their feet "with the preparation of the gospel of peace" (Ephesians 6:15). As painted toes beautify your feet in the natural, peace beautifies our spiritual feet. We are about to learn that not only did Jesus give pedicures; He received them too. His desire is for us to have beautiful, peaceful feet.

BEAUTY INSIDER TIP 1

Every pedicure starts with cleansing

Have you ever read the story where Jesus washed the disciples' feet in John 13 and asked yourself why He did it? They wondered the same thing. In verse 6, Peter asked Jesus, "Are You washing my feet?" Imagine how awkward you would feel if your pastor tried to wash your feet—never mind the man you recognize as the Messiah. Jesus explains to Peter, in verse 8, "If I do not wash you, you have no part with Me." What Peter did not understand is that Jesus loved them so much that He wanted to empower them. Jesus said, "Apart from me you can do nothing" (15:5 NLT). Just like us, the disciples needed to be a part of Jesus for the task they had ahead of them.

Peter didn't need a complete bath; he didn't need a soak in the tub. He just needed his feet washed. That is why Jesus told Peter, "He who is bathed needs only to wash his feet, but is completely clean; and you are clean" (13:10). What he and the other disciples needed was a refreshing. Walking in sandals made for some pretty dirty feet, and they needed all the dust they had gathered throughout the day—and the cares of the world—to be washed off their feet. When you become born again, you are also made clean. First John 1:7 says, "The blood of Jesus Christ His Son cleanses us from all sin." Now, you also only need to have your feet cleaned.

The apostle Paul said that we, the bride of Christ, are "washed by the cleansing of God's word" (Ephesians 5:26 NLT). Through reading, studying, and meditating on the Word of God, our feet become clean. When you spend time with Him in His Word, He washes you from the filth and defilement you have accumulated throughout your daily walk. He cleanses not only your feet, but He scrapes away all the dead, dried, and callused areas of your life. He gives the most peaceful pedicure you will ever receive.

Did you ever get a really good person to do your pedicure, and it seemed as if she knew every pressure point in your feet? It's amazing the difference that treatment makes in the way you feel. Long before the X-ray was invented, doctors could diagnose a person's illness or ailment by examining his or her feet. You see, the Lord created us with pressure points on the bottom of our feet. By touching these pressure points in a certain way, a physician could not only tell if a person was ill, but he was able to determine what part of the body was being affected.

There are times in our lives when we will go through things that will hurt us. These things can cause us to hold on to hatred, bitterness, envy, or pride, which causes hardness in our heart, affecting our walk with the Lord. Especially in these times, we must place our walk in His hands. With the work of His hands, the Great Physician will set you free from every sin, from every hurt, and from every sorrow. He will cause you to walk in peace and victory.

BEAUTY INSIDER TIP 2

Don't forget the oil and enjoy the massage

God is a giver and a receiver, and He expects us to be the same. He told the disciples when He washed their feet, "If I then, your Lord, and Teacher, have washed your feet, you ought also to wash one another's feet" (John 13:14). He will never ask us to do anything that He hasn't already done.

In Luke 7 there is a story where the coin has flipped, and Jesus is the recipient of a pedicure. This foot washing was given by a woman known to be a sinner, and forgiven by Jesus. With a true heart of repentance, Mary washed away the dirt from the feet of Jesus, using nothing but her own hair and tears. But she didn't stop there. She kissed His feet, and—as an act of worship—anointed His feet with oil. The cost of the fragrant oil was a whole year's wage—but it was well worth it to hear Him say, "Your sins are forgiven" (v. 48).

Most pedicures end with oil being massaged into your feet, so I don't think that Mary understood when she poured out her valuable oil, that she was actually anointing Him and preparing Him for the task He had ahead. But she did understand the magnitude of forgiveness she received from Jesus and wanted to give back. When we allow the Lord to anoint us with the oil, He will prepare us for what we have ahead of us.

A Pharisee who witnessed Mary's sacrifice was quick to judge. But unlike him, she had many sins and much to be forgiven, so she loved much. She left behind every hurt, sorrow, and sin at the Lord's feet that day. And He gave her an even greater blessing in exchange: peace. He didn't look at her sin but instead looked at her faith. Jesus assured her, "Your faith has saved you. Go in peace" (v. 50).

Jesus will never command us to do something He hasn't already gifted us with, or given us the ability to do. Imagine telling your children to go somewhere in the car, but you haven't ever given them the keys. When He told Mary to "go in peace," He had already given it to her. He has given us all peace. In John 14:27 He said, "Peace I leave with you, My peace I give to you; not as the world gives do I give to you." Peace is a gift we must choose to give—and choose to receive.

BEAUTY INSIDER TIP 3

Polish it off

Imagine how safe you would feel with a member of the National Guard armed and standing outside your door. That's what the peace of God does for you—protect your mind from external corrupting influences so you can keep your mind focused on God's truth. The peace the Lord has given us will empower us in our fight against the enemy.

Romans 16:20 says, "The God of peace will crush Satan under your feet shortly." In other words, peace will polish off the enemy. Peace is a mighty weapon. It will help you fight in the strongest of battles and become victorious over them. When you're at peace, the enemy is defeated. Philippians 4:6–7 says, "Be anxious for nothing, but in everything by prayer and supplication, with thanksgiving, let your requests be made known to God; and the peace of God, which surpasses all understanding, will guard your hearts and minds through Christ Jesus."

This mighty weapon called peace will also stand guard for you and protect your heart and mind. Walking in God's peace gives us the ability to polish off the enemy and destroy him under our feet. What a comfort to know that the Prince of Peace lives in us.

Daily Reflection

Read John 13:1-17

- What do you think the significance is in washing someone's feet?

Read Luke 7:37-50

- Take a few minutes to sit at the feet of Jesus to worship Him in thanks for your forgiveness.

Read John 14:27

- What are some areas of your life where you need to receive peace?

Application

Just as Jesus gave and received pedicures, we are to give and receive His peace. The next time you hear Ephesians 6:15, which speaks of "having your feet shod with the preparation of the gospel of peace," take a minute to remind yourself of the great gift God has left for you. I suggest that you put down this book and take a few minutes to ask the Lord to help with the areas in which you may struggle. Say ...

> *Here are my feet, Lord. I need you to*
> *apply pressure, massage them, diagnose*
> *me. Make me soft and pliable in your*
> *hands! Show me, Lord, where these hurts*
> *are affecting me. I need you to heal me.*

And then, give peace in return. Remember what Jesus told the multitudes in Matthew 5:9? He said, "Blessed are the peacemakers." Choose today to make peace, seek it, pursue it, walk in it, give it, receive it, and abide in it.

Eyebrow Shaping

Bessie Hicks

*As each one has received a gift, minister it to one another,
as good stewards of the manifold grace of God.*

1 PETER 4:10

Picture this: You're on your way for a much-needed spa day. Your mind is reeling with all the relaxing and refreshing services you're about to indulge in. You're really looking forward to a relaxing facial or full-body massage, followed up by a classic mani-pedi. Are you also looking forward to having your eyebrows shaped? Of course not! Let's face it: No matter which method they use—waxing, threading, or old-fashioned plucking—it's never an enjoyable experience. No one likes the pain that comes with getting her brows shaped, but most of us like them perfect. Now, that being said, let's compare our eyebrows with our spiritual gift. I know that might sound crazy, even for *Beauty Inside Out*, but follow along as we allow the Spirit to teach us these biblical truths.

Everyone is born with eyebrows, right? But, when babies are born, they don't come out with perfectly sculpted eyebrows. They come in stronger as the child develops, but at first they are untamed and unshaped. Did you know everyone is also born with a spiritual gift? The spiritual gifts we are born with are of the same manner: untamed and unshaped. These gifts are given to us for the purpose of doing a work in the kingdom of God—but without shaping and direction, they will become unruly and unattractive to His kingdom. Before we study about our spiritual gifts given to us, I would like you to think about this truth: Every child of God is called to do a work.

BEAUTY INSIDER TIP 1

Eyebrows aren't just for looks

Eyebrows have a purpose, and it's not just to make us look pretty but to keep the sweat and debris from running into our eyes while we work. It's not really glamorous, but it's true. As Christians, sometimes we're more concerned about looking good than doing good. But the Bible says we were created for good works. In the "Manicure" teaching, we learned that if we're willing, God has a work for us to do (Ephesians 2:8–10). However, we don't work to earn salvation; that's a free gift from God. We work because that's what we are created to do. God has created each of us with a purpose in mind. He has gifted us individually, to equip us for the specific assignment He has for us.

"After these things the Lord appointed seventy others also, and sent them two by two before His face into every city and place where He Himself was about to go. Then He said to them, 'The harvest is truly great, but the laborers are few; therefore pray the Lord of the harvest to send out laborers into His harvest'" (Luke 10:1–2). The harvest the Lord is referring to is lost people being brought to salvation.

God is "not willing that any should perish but that all should come to repentance" (2 Peter 3:9). He needs laborers in the field who are willing to put their hand to the plow and, by the sweat of their brow, to do a kingdom work (Luke 9:62). The power and enablement come from the Holy Spirit, and He uses our hands and feet. We represent His body on earth, commissioned to do His work on earth. Humans need God's power, but God uses human power. It's time we get busy about the Father's business.

BEAUTY INSIDER TIP 2

If brows could talk ...

Eyebrows can speak volumes without saying a word; they help us communicate with each other. If the kids are misbehaving in public, we might raise one eyebrow and they will straighten up. But raising both eyebrows could be an expression of joy. But become angry with someone and scowl with your brows as if they are trying to touch, and they will get the hint really quick. In the same way, we can communicate the love of Jesus to a lost and dying world without saying a word.

So many of us think the only way to share the gospel or communicate the love of God is to preach. Don't get me wrong, we need preachers. Romans 10:14 poses the question, "How shall they hear without a preacher?" But preaching isn't the only way to share the message of the gospel. This can be done through serving, giving, and visiting the sick or lonely. Even something as simple as a smile can brighten someone's day. When we think about doing a work for God, most of us think about the big things, but little is much when God is in it. This is where our gifting from God is the most valuable and the most effective.

I once heard the testimony of a man who was prompted, by the Holy Spirit, to give his garbage man a glass of orange juice on a hot summer morning. That simple act of kindness led to that man giving his heart to the Lord. There is a saying that goes, "Preach the gospel everywhere you go and use words if necessary." The apostle Paul said, in 2 Corinthians 3:2, "You are our epistle written in our hearts, known and read by all men." You may be the only Bible someone reads, a living epistle, showing the love of God through your actions. The old saying is true: actions speak louder than words.

BEAUTY INSIDER TIP 3

Eyebrows look best with shaping

We have learned a few things about the function of our eyebrows. Now let's consider them as a feature. Who would have thought brows would become so important in the cosmetic world? Today, they are more popular than ever. I have seen entire salons designated for shaping and styling what, at one time, would have seemed to have been an insignificant feature. I think that one reason eyebrows are so important is they help identify who we are. According to a recent study conducted at

MIT, famous faces are rendered unrecognizable in the absence of eyebrows.

As eyebrows help people identify who we are, so does our spiritual gift. I will use myself as an example: Although I'm a wife, mother, daughter, and sister, most people know me as a Bible teacher. I'm identified by my gift. God has invested gifts in each of us for the purpose of helping us accomplish a work in His kingdom. How we use these gifts is up to us.

I could be teaching a wide variety of things with this teaching gift from the Lord. But as I surrender myself to studying the Word, His masterful hands have shaped me into a Bible teacher to bring Him glory. There are many musicians and vocalists with the gift of exhortation. God may have intended for them to be worship leaders, but instead they're topping the pop music charts with their God-given gifts and talents.

The Bible says in Romans 11:29, "For the gifts and the calling of God are irrevocable." That means God will not take them from you, no matter how you choose to use them. He doesn't change His mind. God has given us free will and wants us to willingly choose to serve Him. However, one day you will stand before the Lord and give an account for how you stewarded what He gave you (1 Corinthians 3:13–15; Matthew 25:14–26).

There are several different categories, or groups, of gifts mentioned in the Word of God. The apostle Paul warns, in 1 Corinthians 12:1, not to be ignorant concerning spiritual gifts. We cannot possibly cover all of them completely in one day, but we are going to try to help you gain a better understanding. It's important to know that all spiritual gifts work together, but in an effort to bring clarity, they can be broken down into three categories: the gifts God has given, the gifts Jesus has given, and the gifts of the Holy Spirit.

Today we will focus on the God-given gifts listed in Romans 12:6–8, otherwise known as the motivational gifts—the motivating force behind how we serve the body of Christ. God has built these gifts in us, and they shape our personalities. These truths are found in both the Old and New Testaments. For example, God spoke, "Before I formed you in the womb I knew you; before you were born I sanctified you; I ordained you a prophet to the nations" (Jeremiah 1:5). God spoke these words about calling Jeremiah to be a prophet. The apostle Paul made a similar statement about himself in Galatians 1:15–16: "God, who separated me from my mother's womb called me through His grace, to reveal His Son in me, that I might preach Him among the Gentiles."

The Bible names other saints whose callings were made clear before they were ever born. John the Baptist was called to be the forerunner for Christ and was filled with the Spirit from his mother's womb (Luke 1). God also had a plan in mind when He created you. He has a purpose you are to fulfill. He chose the family you belong to, the town you live in, and the church you attend. Jeremiah 29:11 says, "For I know the plans I have for you ... plans to prosper you and not harm you, plans to give you hope and a future" (NIV). I want to remind you of this: although God has chosen you to be a gift to the body of Christ, you must choose to follow that calling. He has plans for you—good plans!

Not every believer is created to be an apostle, prophet, evangelist, pastor, or teacher (gifts of the fivefold ministry mentioned in Ephesians 4:11). However, every believer falls into a category of one of the motivational gifts mentioned in Romans 12:6–8 (prophesy, serving, teaching, exhortation, giving, leadership, or showing mercy). Upon further study of these gifts, you should be able to see clearly which ones you can use in the body of Christ. You may have several of these gifts, but one will emerge as your most prominent gift. Paul said, in 1 Corinthians

7:7, "For I wish all men were even as myself. But each one has his own gift from God, one in this manner and another in that."

Again, we'll look at 1 Peter 4:10 to see clearly what we are to do with the gift. "As each one has received a special gift, employ it in serving one another" (NASB). Employ it! Get to work with the gifts God has invested in you. He has given them to you to build up the body of Christ and to advance the kingdom of God. You will find that grace is always mentioned with these gifts, for by grace we receive them as gifts; they are not something we've earned. Love is also mentioned in connection with these gifts; through His love, we serve one another—or it profits nothing (1 Corinthians 13:3).

Daily Reflection

Read Romans 12:3-8

- What are the seven gifts given by God?

Read Ephesians 4:7-11

- What are the five gifts given by Jesus?

Read 1 Corinthians 12:7-11

- What are the nine gifts given by the Holy Spirit?

Application

Just as you're born with eyebrows, you are born with a gift inside of you. No matter how unruly or unshaped your eyebrows grow, you never completely remove them (although I have seen people do this, and it's not very attractive). You shape your eyebrows into something beautiful that frames your eyes and face. Likewise, God wants to shape you, removing the wild hair or anything in us that's not like Him. He wants to shape and perfect the gift that He has placed in you.

Don't be afraid of losing yourself when you surrender to God. You will always be you. The gifts He has given you were there from the beginning. They are what motivate you to act and do the things you do. They are what make you exceptional and unique. Allow God to shape and mold you into the greatest, most beautiful person He created you to be.

DAY 19

Facial

Theresa Smith

*So the L*ORD *spoke to Moses face to face,*
as a man speaks to his friend.

EXODUS 33:11

Have you ever been a little bit jealous of someone's beautiful skin? That person whose face seems to glow, even when she just rolled out of bed? Chances are she is faithful in caring for her skin. Nothing can replace the results that can be seen by someone who is consistent with her daily skin routine. A lot of times, even though we want the same results, we don't want to spend what's necessary to achieve that glow. Those who have been faithful will age more gracefully than those who have not. Even so, everyone can benefit from professional help; a good facial can still improve even the most beautiful skin in the world. As important as daily care may be, there is nothing like the quick work that can be done when we seek professional help. Experts can assess and treat things we can't manage on our own. They will help us achieve our goals much faster.

The word *facial*, according to *Merriam-Webster's Dictionary*, means "of or relating to the face." An aesthetician, or a skin care specialist, can see things in your skin that you might not. This gives her an advantage in pinpointing your problem areas. There are three ways she's able to do this: special equipment, education, and experience. But she must also come face-to-face with her client. When it comes to our spiritual walk, there are three things we can come face-to-face with that will make a noticeable difference in our lives: Jesus Himself, His church assembly, and His ministers.

Just as we can't replace consistent daily skin care, nothing can take the place of our daily walk with the Lord. Praying every day—in addition to studying and applying the Word of God—cleanses us from our sins. This purification process allows us to cast off the flesh and receive fresh oil from the Holy Spirit. You can always recognize those who spend time in the presence of the Lord. They will look, walk, and talk differently than those who neglect their personal time with God.

BEAUTY INSIDER TIP 1

We meet Jesus face-to-face

Have you ever heard this saying: "never the same in Jesus' name"? I can remember very clearly the times in my life when I have met with the Master, and I was never the same. It wasn't just a feeling or an emotion; it was a true change. I grew up in church, knowing and doing the things of the Lord. But it wasn't until I met Him face-to-face that I really begin to walk with Him. I thought I knew Him before, but I had no idea I really didn't.

I can remember the day I truly met Jesus, and the weeks and months that followed, as if it were yesterday. When I was filled with His Spirit, everything about me changed—my desires, the company I kept, and how I spent my time. My stomach actually burned like fire for weeks after this experience. Before I met Him face-to-face, I had been praying for a long time for Him to show me He was real. He is so faithful to us and His Word that He heard my cry and met me where I was at, when I least expected it. He promises in His Word, "You will seek Me and find Me, when you search for Me with all your heart" (Jeremiah 29:13).

Moses spent forty days and forty nights face-to-face with God receiving instruction for His people (Exodus 34:29–35). When he came down from the mountain, his skin was shining (v. 29). It was physically evident to all that he had been in the presence of God! When we come face-to-face with God, it will also be evident to the world. He will not only give us the instructions that we need, but He will also cause us to shine like Him. If we allow Him to, He can instantly remove impurities, struggles, or issues as we soak in His presence. Just as a facial shouldn't be a onetime thing, this face-to-face experience with the Lord shouldn't be just a onetime thing. And, like a facial, it most likely won't be a daily thing either.

Seeking the face of God will take away impurities and bring about beauty, healing, and change. I went through a time of breakouts on my skin, so I started to get a facial once a month and follow my aesthetician's instructions. The results were amazing! My skin has changed since then, but I still need a facial every so often. It's the same with the Lord. When you find yourself having trouble or showing some unpleasantness in your spirit, seek the face of God. He is sure to leave you glowing and radiant after a time in His presence.

BEAUTY INSIDER TIP 2

The church sheds light

After you've been relaxing a while, your aesthetician will shine a very bright light on your face and examine your skin with a magnifying mirror that reveals every flaw. This is by far my least favorite part of the facial. It's always a little awkward hearing her sighs and the little comments she makes while looking at my face with one of those devices. Like, "Hmmm," "oh," or "huh?" It makes you wonder, *What is she actually seeing?* Maybe you have clogged pores, or maybe you have thrown the poor woman into shock because she is seeing the damage from your years of baking in the sun.

That blue light reveals everything (in the natural). In the spirit realm, walking in the light (1 John 1:7) exposes things—things that cannot be seen without close examination. Verse 7 continues, "If we walk in the light as [God] is in the light, we have fellowship with one another, and the blood of Jesus ... cleanses us from all sin." It's so important for us to gather together in the presence of His Spirit, where the teaching and preaching of His Word can shed light on our hearts and minds.

The benefits of regular church attendance can be amazing. There are times in my personal life when I have been wrestling with something all week, and I just can't seem to shake it or find the answer. When I finally make it to the house of God, and members of His body of believers are worshiping together, instantly I know that thing can be resolved.

Jesus promises us, "Where two or three are gathered together in My name, I am there in the midst of them" (Matthew 18:20). We also know that "where the Spirit of the Lord is, there is liberty" (2 Corinthians 3:17). In other words, if we gather together with God's people in Jesus' name, He is always there. And if He is there, freedom is there. It's really that simple.

BEAUTY INSIDER TIP 3

Ministers help us see our true reflection

We can see our reflections in a mirror, but who stands in front of a mirror all day? Yes, I know some do more than others, and it's necessary because that's the only way for you to see yourself. But the truth is, other people see you more often than you see yourself. And most of the time, we have a distorted perception of what we look like. We tend to focus on the few flaws we think we have, and that can become all that we see.

The truth is, other people see us more often than we see ourselves. When someone looks into your face, they can clearly see you. It's always helpful, but not fun, when a friend points out that you have food on your face or that your mascara is running. But what about the times when it's your good features they see?

I'm thankful for my friends. If it wasn't for them pointing out my good qualities, I would constantly walk around feeling condemned. Like these friends, God has given us gifts in church (Romans 12:3–8; Ephesians 4:11; 1 Corinthians 12:7–11). And believe it or not, these gifts are people. Ministers are servants of God set in place to see your good features, edify you, draw out the gifts inside of you, and help you to get rid of the "not so good."

Proverbs 13:20 tells us, "He who walks with wise men will be wise." Wise, experienced, Spirit-filled ministers—people full of love, wisdom, and godly advice—can counsel us on the things we can change to draw us closer to God. They can also provoke us "to love and good works," as Hebrews 10:24 says (ESV). Likewise, we should be the same toward our fellow believers, stirring up the good in our brothers and sisters in Christ and building one another up with confidence in the Lord.

King Solomon, perhaps the wisest person of all time, wrote, "As iron sharpens iron, so a man sharpens the countenance of his friend" (Proverbs 27:17). One of the ways *Strong's Concordance* defines *countenance* is "face." This reminds me that when a sword is sharpened, it's shiny—just how we look after a facial and how we should look after receiving godly counsel.

Daily Reflection

Read Exodus 34:29-35

- What caused Moses' face to shine?

Read Ecclesiastes 4:10-12

- Why is it important to have one another?

Read Hebrews 10:24-25

- What does the writer implore us to do and not do?

Application

When you spend time in fellowship with the Lord, your church, and its ministers, your face will begin to glow. As you have allowed the wisdom of those around you to edify you and build you up, you will walk with more confidence because you know you have the glow. Ask God to send you people who are wiser than you and who have more experience than you in the Lord. Link yourself to them, follow their counsel, then do the same for someone else.

DAY 20

Massage

Laura Wharton, Sandy Wharton, & Sadie Rose

Be my strong refuge,
to which I may resort continually.

PSALM 71:3

We can't leave our week at the spa without a much-needed massage. Now, picture yourself at a resort the Lord has made for you; a refuge from stress. The sight of it is so beautiful it takes your breath away. As you walk through the doors, you see a sign hanging on the wall that says:

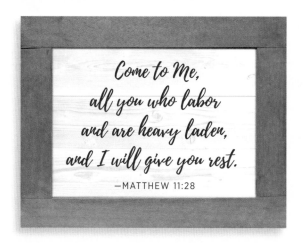

Come to Me,
all you who labor
and are heavy laden,
and I will give you rest.

—MATTHEW 11:28

God knows you are long overdue for a rest. The cares of the world and of everyday life have you feeling tense and weighed down. As you stand there reading the sign, a relaxing aroma fills you with an overwhelming sense of peace. You can feel His presence—and you know in your heart everything is going to be all right.

Spas use scents (aromatherapy) for the purpose of setting an inviting and comforting surrounding. This is actually a biblical principle; incense was used as an act of worship, to invite the presence of God. The smell became a sweet fragrance to the Lord and created an atmosphere, welcoming His presence to come down and dwell. This principle kind of reminds me (Laura) of my grandmother. I love the smell of eucalyptus till this day—because if I stayed with her for any length of time, I would come away smelling like it. The rest of my family could always tell when I had been with her. It kind of makes me wonder, *When I spend time in the presence of the Lord, is it noticeable to others?*

BEAUTY INSIDER TIP 1

Setting the atmosphere

When Jesus comes and dwells among us through worship, His scent lingers with us, which makes us more Christlike and benefits those around us. It should become difficult for the world to make a distinction between us and Jesus. Second Corinthians 2:14 says, "He uses us to spread the knowledge of Christ everywhere, like a sweet perfume" (NLT). In Song of Solomon 3:6, Jesus is described as "coming out of the wilderness like pillars of smoke, perfumed with frankincense and myrrh." Imagine what a welcome relief it would be for a person who has been in the wilderness for a while to feel the presence of Jesus. When we live in a spirit of worship, that presence is always with us, and He changes the atmosphere.

A story is told about Smith Wigglesworth, a famous evangelist from the 1800s. The presence of God was so strong around him, people would start to cry as he walked by, asking him what they needed to do to be saved. Right then and there, the lost and the undone would give their hearts to the Lord. This is how we should be operating in the kingdom. The presence of our Lord, on and in us, should draw the lost and the unsaved to us, so we can point them to Jesus. His presence is all that is needed to cause even the hardest of sinners to turn and repent.

In addition to scents, another way a spa sets the atmosphere is by putting you in the right attire. Like many massage therapists would do, God hands you a clean robe. This is not just your average terrycloth bathrobe. It's made of the most valuable white linen ever created—it's a robe of righteousness. In exchange for casting off your old garments, you receive your robe of righteousness. "Concerning your former conduct," Paul writes in Ephesians 4:22–24, "be renewed in the spirit of your mind, and ... put on the new man which was created according to God, in true righteousness and holiness."

BEAUTY INSIDER TIP 2

Deep-tissue issues

I'm going to be real for a few minutes. I (Sadie) was a little hesitant about working on today's devotion and put it off for a while. The reason is because I have never had an actual full-body massage. One morning, the Lord started to show me this because my body was aching from a hard workout I had done a few days before. I wanted so badly to go for a massage and get all the kinks and knots worked out, but my pride wouldn't allow it. Instead, I sat at home in pain.

I had gone to get a massage in the past but ended up backing out and getting a neck massage and facial instead. We know a facial is necessary for keeping away blemishes, but it wasn't what I needed that particular day. I just couldn't bring myself to let someone massage my whole body. The reason stems from an underlying issue (yes, this is about to get deep). Even though I eat healthy now, years of yo-yo dieting and not exercising have left me in an awful shape, and I'm ashamed to get a massage. The Lord used my own example to show me the condition of the body of Christ.

The members of the church make up the whole body, but some refuse to allow the Lord to work out their problem areas. This can stem from three reasons: they are too full of pride, they are too full of shame, or they fear it will hurt. We would all love for the heads of our church to be worked on: pastors, preachers, evangelists, and board members ... or even the neck and shoulders: the worship team, deacons, and Sunday school teachers. But don't come near the rest of the body! There's too much shame to uncover and too much pain that has been buried for years.

Our pride, fear, and shame will not allow for the Lord to reach those deep-tissue issues, because we can't bear to be touched. But we must understand what the Word of God teaches about believers: As the body of Christ, we are "joined and knit together by what every joint supplies" (Ephesians 4:16). Focusing on just one area causes imbalance in the body and throws off the equilibrium of the church. If we want to function properly as a body, we need to allow the Lord to work out the kinks in every single joint.

When I needed the massage on my back, but only let her massage my neck, my neck felt great. The problem was, my back was still in terrible pain. Although I only had pain in one area, my entire body was affected. I was imbalanced and found it difficult to accomplish simple tasks. I couldn't even turn over in bed, and struggled to get up from a lying-down position. I was like a cast-down sheep—but praise God for the Good Shepherd, who always looks after His flock!

BEAUTY INSIDER TIP 3

Restored and renewed

Speaking of sheep, I want to take a few minutes to talk about them. I know we're supposed to be at the spa, but bear with me for a minute. When a sheep lies on its back, it can't get back up. (This is what a shepherd refers to as being *cast down*.) It's actually a very pathetic sight. The sheep lies there with its legs in the air, struggling to stand, which leaves it completely helpless against predators—kind of like I was with my back out. As Christians, we too can become cast down when we allow worry, hurt, fear, bitterness, and temptation to come into our lives.

This can happen to a sheep for a few different reasons. One could be because the sheep became too fat. We can relate that to pride, which causes us to become puffed up. Another is because it became weighed down. A sheep's wool is very heavy—and when dirt, debris, water, or mud build up, it can topple over, like when we get weighed down with the cares of the world. A third reason for this to happen is because the sheep has become too comfortable with where it's at. We as Christians sometimes feel as if we've arrived, which gives us a tendency to become passive in our walk with the Lord. Instead of pressing in to Him, we roll over—leaving us open for an attack from the enemy.

Here's the good news: When a sheep gets in this position, the shepherd goes out to find it (Matthew 18:12). He gently and tenderly turns it over and lifts it onto its feet. He holds his precious sheep up, because it has lost its balance, and begins to massage its legs. This can be a little uncomfortable to the sheep at first, as the blood begins to flow back into its sleeping limbs. But as he continues to gently knead and apply pressure to the muscles, he works out every knot, kink, and painful spot until the sheep is restored to an upright position with the strength to stand and walk by the shepherd's side (Psalm 23:3-4).

King David, being a shepherd boy, was very familiar with this. Just like us, he found himself in a cast-down state at times. He knew where his hope came from and how he could become restored and renewed. "Why are you cast down, O my soul? And why are you disquieted within me? Hope in God; for I shall yet praise Him, the help of my countenance and my God" (Psalm 43:5). He knew God was his Shepherd and that when his Shepherd found him, He would gently massage him until he was completely restored.

If we can grasp the concept of the Lord as our Shepherd, we have hope. God can help us get rid of pride or shame and regain strength and balance. Old hurts are healed; bondages are broken; and things like bitterness, anger, strife, and hopelessness all fall away.

Daily Reflection

Read Ephesians 4:22-24

- Why do you think Paul says to "put off ... the old man" (v. 22)?

Read Ephesians 4:15-16

- Why is it important for us to allow the Lord to work on our deep-tissue issues?

Read Psalm 23

- Will you allow the Lord to be your Shepherd today?

Application

I would like to end this study by telling you that I went and got that massage, and I feel much better. But that wouldn't be the truth. The truth is, I am sitting here with my back in pain as I write. In the natural, I have been very stubborn—more like a goat than a sheep. Don't operate in the spiritual as I have in the natural. Instead, go to the resort of the Shepherd. Enter into His presence with a heart of worship and allow Him to restore you. As He places the white robe of His righteousness on you, He will heal your every hurt, work out every kink, and stand you in an upright position so you can walk by His side.

DAY 21

Reflection and Direction

Sadie Rose

But we all, with unveiled face, beholding as in a mirror the glory of the Lord, are bing transformed into the same image from glory to glory, just as by the Spirit of the Lord.

2 CORINTHIANS 3:18

Congratulations! You have made it to the twenty-first day of your devotions. Research has proven that is the amount of time it takes to form a new habit. Now that you have officially created this new routine of time in the Word, you should be able to continue for the rest of your life. We are hoping by now you are feeling refreshed and renewed in your natural body and in your spirit. But, like every beauty routine, spiritual growth is a continual process. If you neglect your skin, hair, or face, it becomes apparent to all around you. Studying the Bible is no different. Neglecting your time with the Lord will eventually become obvious to all who see you.

You will have to apply the Word of God to every need and every situation that should arise. The best way to do that is by having the Word hidden in your heart instead of scrambling at the last minute to search for a verse that ministers to your need. Renewing your mind again and again by the washing of the water of the Word will not only benefit you but your family, friends, church, and the world around you.

BEAUTY INSIDER TIP 1

Look in the mirror

In the introduction to *Beauty Inside Out*, we talked about a beautiful young girl named Esther and all the lavish treatments she underwent in hopes of becoming the next queen. She found favor with the king above all the other women and became his bride. One of my favorite things about this shining star is that all her pampering and beautifying did not go to waste. Esther could have chosen to live a pampered life in the lap of luxury, but instead she used her royal position to influence the king. Because of her selflessness, she saved the entire race of her own people. We are all in the same position as Esther. Each one of us has undergone this time of preparation, and it's not without purpose.

Do you know anyone who goes through such extreme measures to make herself beautiful, just to sit at home? There are people out there who need us. They need to feel the presence of God we carry and experience the love of God as we have had the privilege of feeling. Here's how you can help: As you would look in the mirror before going out the door, also look in the mirror of the Word before you face the world. Reflect upon what it says and make certain it's being applied properly. Then, go out the door and be a witness. You may be the only Bible someone will ever read. In 2 Corinthians 3:2, the apostle Paul tells the readers, "You are our epistle written in our hearts, known and read by all men."

You may be thinking to yourself that you didn't read this book because you wanted to preach; you just desired to learn the Word. Too late! As we learned throughout these past weeks, preaching is proclaiming the gospel, and we are all called to share the good news. Just before Jesus ascended to the Father, He left every believer with what is known as the Great Commission: "Go into all the world and preach the gospel to every creature" (Mark 16:15).

If you have never considered yourself an Esther, think again. We were all born "for such a time as this" (Esther 4:14). We are fortunate enough to have an even greater blessing than she did. She went into the king without knowing what the outcome would be—but we have the promises of God to stand on. "For I know the thoughts I have toward you, says the Lord, thoughts of peace and not of evil, to give you a future and a hope" (Jeremiah 29:11).

BEAUTY INSIDER TIP 2

Do it again

As you know, Esther was granted her petition from the king, and the Jews were saved from annihilation. But did you know what happened next? After the Jews were saved and the evil Haman was killed, the king came to Esther with a question. He asked her what would she like him to do next, now that her petition was answered. He said, "It shall be done" (Esther 9:12). She could have asked for countless things—but as we know, that's not her style. Esther's answer was, "Do it again tomorrow according to today's decree" (v. 13). I would have imagined that after the stress of it all, she would have been tired and ready to relax and enjoy the comforts of the palace. But Esther had tasted victory—and she wasn't ready to back down.

We have a King who is also ready to grant our petitions. Jesus said in John 15:7, "If you abide in Me, and My words abide in you, you will ask what you desire, and it shall be done for you." We can bring our requests before Him, and He is faithful to answer.

BEAUTY INSIDER TIP 3

What's your "before and after"?

Before you began this study, hopefully you answered the questions in the beauty questionnaire, as a type of before-and-after assessment. Now return to the questions and reevaluate your answers. You should see some improvement. Don't be discouraged if you don't see a dramatic difference. Four weeks is actually not very long—considering this is a lifelong change. If you're seeing some change, you're doing well. Chances are, you will notice the differences before anyone else does. You may find yourself excited about waking up a bit earlier; or picking up your Bible instead of shopping online when you're having your cup of coffee. But the changes in you will eventually become apparent to your family, your friends, and then those around you.

I would like to give you a little advice: Your relationship with the Lord is not to be compared to anyone else's. You may have a sister or a friend you have been doing the study with, and you're seeing more changes in her than you are in yourself. It's okay. Don't let that get you down. The apostle Paul warns us in 2 Corinthians 10:12 not to compare ourselves to each other. The Christian life is not a competition. As long as you are walking with Jesus, moving forward (not going backward or standing still), you're doing well. One day in the presence of the King is better than a thousand without Him (Psalm 84:10).

Daily Reflection

Read Mark 16:15

- Are you willing to accept the Great Commission?

Read Esther 9:12-15

- Will your request to the King make a difference in the life of another?

Read your favorite chapter in the Bible

- Ask the Lord what part of it He would like you to share with someone today.

Application

Take a page from Esther's book—keep pressing in and keep moving forward. The Lord will continue to show you things as long as you continue to study. Yes, the Lord has blessed us with kingdom living, but it's not so we can live the high life while our people are perishing all around us. We were born for such a time as this. Let the Holy Spirit guide you on where to begin.

If you would like to study other portions of Scripture, there are plenty of resources available. You can choose ones that are based on a subject (love, deliverance, healing, peace), a person in the Bible (Jesus, David, Esther, Paul), or maybe the ministry gifts (apostle, prophet, evangelist, pastor, teacher). There are countless things to study in the Word of God, so I would suggest starting with something that applies to your current situation. Study it, meditate on the Scriptures, ask the Lord to reveal them to you, and then do it again.

Apply the Word. Apply the Word. Apply the Word. You will never be able to apply the Word unless you know the Word. The only way to know the Word is to study the Word. And studying the Word will make you a "Beauty Inside Out"!

Receiving the Baptism of the Holy Spirit

These are a few simple truths that will help you receive the baptism of the Holy Spirit:

1. Your heavenly Father wants you to receive the baptism of the Holy Spirit. It is a gift—and, like salvation, it can't be earned. It must be received by faith. He has already given the Holy Spirit; you just need to receive the baptism. You do not need to beg; only ask and believe!

   "If you then, being evil, know how to give good gifts to your children, how much more will your heavenly Father give the Holy Spirit to those who ask Him!" (Luke 11:13)

2. Anyone who is saved can receive the baptism of the Holy Spirit.

   Then Peter said to them, "Repent, and let every one of you be baptized in the name of Jesus Christ for the remission of sins; and you shall receive the gift of the Holy Spirit." (Acts 2:38)

3. There are many different examples in Scripture of believers receiving the Spirit's baptism. Generally, they
received this baptism when a Spirit-filled believer laid
hands on them. However, in Acts 10, the Bible states
that while they were listening to Peter preach, the
Gentiles were saved and were baptized in the Spirit,
with the evidence of speaking in tongues.

4. If you desire to receive the baptism of the Spirit,
simply ask Jesus to baptize you with the Holy Spirit.
You can receive this baptism right where you are. I
know countless testimonies of people receiving the
gift while alone, simply by asking God in faith. My
husband received the baptism of the Holy Spirit while
he was alone, crying out to God.

> While Peter was still speaking these
> words, the Holy Spirit fell upon all
> those who heard the word. And those
> of the circumcision who believed were
> astonished, as many as came with
> Peter, because of the gift of the Holy
> Spirit had been poured out on the
> Gentiles also. For they heard them
> speak with tongues and magnify God.
> (Acts 10:44–46)

5. You will not need to wonder if you have received the
baptism of the Spirit because the initial evidence
is speaking in tongues. Some people think the Holy
Spirit will just take over your tongue and speak for
you, but the Holy Spirit will speak through you. He
will give you the utterance; however, you will have to

open your mouth by faith and speak. Your heavenly language may only be a few syllables at first; but as you continue to speak, it will flow more and more.

The baptism of the Holy Spirit will empower you to be a witness for the Lord and accomplish everything He has called you to do. If you're ready, don't wait. Ask God in faith, believing that He will act. It's as simple as saying, "Lord, baptize me with your power from on high. I receive the gift of the Holy Spirit." Then open your mouth and begin to speak in your heavenly language by faith. It can be that easy—and He will fill you.

If you feel more comfortable having a Spirit-filled believer lay hands on you and pray, then by all means, do so. The Lord is waiting to give you His gift, which can transform your walk with Him; your ministry; and your life.

Acknowledgments

There are so many people I want to thank for being a part of *Beauty Inside Out.* I want to start by thanking the Lord for the vision and the Holy Spirit for being my helper, teacher, and guide. Without Him I can do nothing!

I'm so grateful for my husband, who allows me to do everything the Lord puts in my heart; and my children, who've stood behind me every step of the way. My family has been extremely patient with me while I poured hours into the book. Sometimes they didn't get the attention they're used to, but they didn't say a word. What a blessing to have a husband and children who love and serve the Lord!

I'm overwhelmed with the team of women God has given me at Love His Word Ministries. When I shared the vision with them, they didn't hesitate at all but picked it up and ran with it. They trusted me, even though none of us had ever done anything like this before. We learned together through the Holy Spirit— and I wouldn't change that experience for anything in the world. I can't thank them enough for how much prayer, fasting, time, and energy they have poured into seeing the vision come to pass. I could have never done it without them.

About the Author

Bessie Hicks is an evangelist, minister, and anointed teacher of the Word of God, to women across the country. She lives in Chester, Virginia, where she founded and serves as head of Love His Word Ministries. Her heart's desire is to provoke a love for the Word of God in the hearts of women around the world.

Bessie and her husband, Willy, have a wonderful son and two beautiful daughters, and the Lord has recently blessed them with an amazing new daughter-in-law. They all have a deep love for the Word of God and have been faithful in ministry to the Lord at their local church—Cornerstone Faith Assembly (in Richmond, Virginia)—for the past twenty years.

The verse on which Bessie has based her life and ministry is found in the book of Psalms: "Thy word have I hid in mine heart, that I might not sin against thee" (Psalm 119:11 KJV).